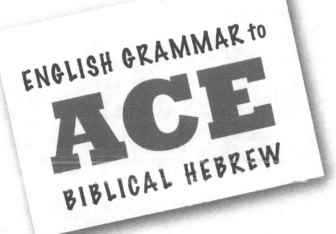

MILES V. VAN PELT

ZONDERVAN

English Grammar to Ace Biblical Hebrew
Copyright © 2010 by Miles V. Van Pelt

Requests for information should be addressed to:
Zondervan, 3900 *Sparks Drive SE, Grand Rapids, Michigan* 49546

Library of Congress Cataloging-in-Publication Data

Van Pelt, Miles V., 1969-
    English grammar to ace biblical Hebrew / Miles V. Van Pelt.
      p. cm.
    Text in English; some examples in English and Hebrew.
    ISBN 978-0-310-31831-6 (pbk.)
      1. English language — Textbooks for foreign speakers — Hebrew.
    2. English language — Grammar, Comparative — Hebrew. 3. Hebrew
language — Grammar, Comparative — English. I. Title.
PE1130.H5V35 2010
428.2'4924--dc22   2009040176

Any Internet addresses (websites, blogs, etc.) and telephone numbers printed in this book are offered as a resource. They are not intended in any way to be or imply an endorsement by Zondervan, nor does Zondervan vouch for the content of these sites and numbers for the life of this book.

Cover design: Mark Veldheer
Interior design: Miles V. Van Pelt

Printed in the United States of America

For Hardy Warren
former reprobate, now saint
my friend

Contents

Acknowledgments

Thanks to Verlyn Verbrugge and the Zondervan team. It is always a pleasure to work with friends. Our collaborations now span eighteen years. I still remember the first project; editing Bill's analytical Greek lexicon in 1991, and getting paid with books. Those were the days!

There were several people who read this book at various stages in the process. My wife, Laurie, even in the midst of her busy schedule, took time to read several chapters for me. It was also encouraging to have my son Ben help with the editing. He can outspell me any day of the week (at age eleven!), and he made many helpful suggestions. Thanks are also due to Jonathan Kiel and Josh Walker, my friends and faithful teaching assistants. Not only did they help with editing, but they also shouldered a heavy work load during the 2009 summer Greek courses at RTS, freeing me to write in the afternoons. Thanks also to Bob Banning for his expertise in English grammar.

Thanks to Reformed Theological Seminary in Jackson, Mississippi, for providing the environment to study, teach, and write. RTS is a great place to work. Thanks also to my family: Laurie, Ben, Kacie, Madie, and Max. You provide the perfect context for the work of my calling. Together we give thanks to our Lord.

כִּי טוֹב יהוה לְעוֹלָם חַסְדּוֹ

Introduction

WHY THIS BOOK?

I have the uncommon privilege of teaching all three biblical languages at Reformed Theological Seminary in Jackson, Mississippi. In each course, I continue to observe that students are not simply struggling to learn Hebrew, Aramaic, or Greek; they are also struggling to learn English. Now, let's be clear. Most of my students already speak the English language, and so they are not struggling to communicate in English, or even to understand English vocabulary. Rather, I see my students struggling with the basic concepts of English grammar. The categories of pronoun and antecedent, direct and indirect object, transitive and intransitive, continue to stupefy even the most enthusiastic student. So I often find myself teaching a fourth foreign language in the classroom, the language of English grammar.

A knowledge of both English and Hebrew grammar is essential for your studies. A foreign language like Hebrew consists of more than just foreign words. It also contains foreign grammar and syntax. Good translations require more than the translation of words. They also require the translation of grammar and syntax. You will discover that translating a Hebrew word into an English word is not that difficult. Translating a Hebrew sentence into an English sentence, however, is much more difficult. Translating sentences requires the translation of grammar and syntax. If your knowledge of English grammar is poor, then your ability to translate Hebrew into English will suffer. And, if you can't translate Hebrew into English, then your ability to understand and interpret the biblical text will be hindered, and this is what we want to avoid.

So, this little book is intended to provide Hebrew students with a very basic introduction to English grammar. Please understand, however, that this introduction is not comprehensive, but rather selective. The grammatical presentations that follow are limited and shaped by the needs of those students who are working to learn biblical Hebrew.

It is also worth noting that many students who study biblical languages in an English-speaking context may not be native speakers. Many of my students, for example, are from South Korea or Africa. I hope that this book will serve their needs too.

HOW TO USE THIS BOOK

Depending on your needs, there are a number of different ways in which this book may be used. One approach would be to read the entire book and complete the exercises in each chapter before you begin working through a Hebrew grammar. This approach would provide a comprehensive summary of English grammatical concepts necessary for the study of Hebrew grammar.

Another option would be to work through the nominal material in chapters 1–7 of this book and then to work through the nominal material in a Hebrew grammar, such as *Basics of Biblical Hebrew* (abbreviated *BBH*) or any other standard Hebrew grammar. After the nominal material is completed, students could tackle the verbal material in chapters 8–14 in preparation for studying the Hebrew verbal system.

Finally, you may have noticed that each chapter listed in the table of contents contains references to chapters in *BBH*. You can simply work through this book in conjunction with the study of Hebrew, topic by topic. But this is simply another suggestion. The design of the book and the references contained within each of the chapters are intended to provide maximum flexibility and adaptability.

TIPS FOR STUDYING HEBREW

If you are preparing to learn biblical Hebrew, allow me to offer a few words of language learning wisdom. I have watched many students succeed and others fail. There are some common characteristics for both groups. If you would like to succeed, consider the following:

1. **Find a study group!** Don't isolate yourself. The power of accountability, encouragement, and friendship in the context of language study must not be underestimated. Help others!

2. **Study regularly!** It is better to study a little bit every day than all day on Friday. You brain was made to use language every day. So use it every day. Regular study quickly turns short term memory into long term memory. Don't cram!

3. **Study early!** Your brain simply works better early in the morning. You will absorb more information and keep it longer if you study early in the morning. It is simply more efficient. There are also fewer distractions, especially at 5:00 AM.

4. **Exercise!** Your brain and your body are connected. Regular exercise will increase your brain's ability to learn. Avoid "scholar's body." It's not pretty!

5. **Sleep!** No problem here, right? The rigors of language learning will tax your mind and so you will need extra sleep. Perhaps you will dream in Hebrew.

ADDITIONAL HEBREW RESOURCES

When it comes to Hebrew language resources, Zonder-van offers the most comprehensive set of language learning tools. I like to think of it as the "no excuse" system. These resources are listed below. Three cheers for Zondervan!

Basics of Biblical Hebrew: Grammar
Gary D. Pratico and Miles V. Van Pelt

Basics of Biblical Hebrew: Workbook
Gary D. Pratico and Miles V. Van Pelt

Biblical Hebrew Charts
Miles V. Van Pelt and Gary D. Pratico

Zondervan Get an A! Study Guides: Biblical Hebrew
Miles V. Van Pelt and Gary D. Pratico

The Vocabulary Guide to Biblical Hebrew
Miles V. Van Pelt and Gary D. Pratico

Hebrew Vocabulary Cards
Miles V. Van Pelt and Gary D. Pratico

Basics of Biblical Hebrew Vocabulary Audio
Miles V. Van Pelt and Gary D. Pratico
Read by Jonathan T. Pennington

Graded Reader of Biblical Hebrew:
A Guide to Reading the Hebrew Bible
Miles V. Van Pelt and Gary D. Pratico

A Reader's Hebrew Bible
A. Philip Brown II and Bryan W. Smith

ALPHABET:
Time to Learn about Your ABCs

ANCIENT TECHNOLOGY

Some of us can remember when computers filled entire rooms and cost hundreds of thousands of dollars to build. In those days, computers were available only to the elite in business, government, or education. Today, however, computers are common, handheld, and affordable. Small children run around with computers more powerful than those that sent the first man to the moon. In some ways, the history of writing is not that different from the history of the modern computer.

Prior to the invention of the alphabet about 4,000 years ago, writing systems were large and cumbersome, consisting of hundreds or even thousands of different written symbols. Due to the complexity of writing systems like this, their use was often restricted to scribes for conducting business or to priests for religious purposes. The ancient Egyptian writing system, for example, commonly known as hieroglyphics, consists of hundreds of different symbols, each representing a different word. This system of writing is called a **logography** and is represented today by traditional Chinese, which utilizes thousands of different written symbols. In a system like this, a single sign could represent a noun like "human."

In addition to the logographic writing system, there was also the **syllabary**, the symbols of which represent different syllables.[1] An example of a syllabic writing system is Akkadian (one of the languages Daniel would have learned in Babylon). There are over 200 basic signs in Akkadian, each of which represents a different syllable.[2] In a writing system like this one, the noun "human" would have been written with two symbols, one for the syllable "hu" and another for the syllable "man."

As you might imagine, the memorization of hundreds or even thousands of different written symbols for a single language would overwhelm just about anybody. With an **alphabet**, however, only a handful of written symbols are required to represent a spoken language.

In English there are twenty-six letters in the alphabet, and in Hebrew there are only twenty-three letters (*BBH* 1.1). Alphabets are compact, flexible, and powerful. The reduction of a written system of language to fewer than thirty characters has certainly expanded the potential for literacy.

---

1.   A syllable is a combination of consonant and vowel sounds, the combinations of which form words (*BBH* 3.1).

2.   David Marcus, *A Manual of Akkadian* (Lanham, MD: University Press of America, 1978), 111–25.

Even today, small children learn the English alphabet with little trouble. This single alphabet, however, can be used to create hundreds of thousands of words in English as well as many other languages such as Spanish, German, and French.

ENGLISH AND HEBREW ALPHABETS

Before you begin a study of the Hebrew alphabet, it is a good idea first to consider the English alphabet. Most of what follows you already know intuitively. However, consideration of the English alphabet will help you to understand related aspects of the Hebrew alphabet.

First, the English alphabet consists of twenty-six letters, but not all letters were created equal. In English there are twenty-one consonants and five vowels – a, e, i, o, and u. One of these consonants, the letter y, can also function as a vowel. For example, the y in "yellow" functions as a consonant, but the y in "silly" functions as a vowel. In the Hebrew alphabet, there are twenty-three consonants, but no vowels (*BBH* 2.1). That's right, no vowels![3] There are, however, three Hebrew consonants that can be used to indicate vowels in certain contexts (ה, ו, and י). When used as vowel indicators, they are called "vowel letters" (see chapter 2 and *BBH* 2.7).

Second, the English alphabet (derived from Latin) and the Hebrew alphabet (derived from Aramaic) use completely different sets of written symbols. For example, the English m and the Hebrew מ (called "Mem") represent the same basic sound but use different symbols to represent that sound. In other words, you could write English using Hebrew letters or Hebrew using English characters. I could spell the English

---

3.   A more technical designation for an alphabetic writing system without vowels is abjad.

noun "dog" as דֹּג using Hebrew letters or I could spell the
Hebrew noun כֶּלֶב (meaning "dog") with English letters as
"kelev." When learning another language like Spanish, one
finds that the written symbols are the same but the words
are different. In Hebrew, both the alphabetic symbols and
the actual words or vocabulary are different. Don't worry
too much about this. It may seem complicated right now, but
your brain is hardwired to understand, interpret, and use
language. That's just how God made you.

Third, the English alphabet is written from left to right
but the Hebrew alphabet is written from right to left (*BBH*
1.3). Try opening up to Genesis in the Hebrew Bible and
your first instinct will be wrong. In the Hebrew Bible, Genesis is located in what looks to us like the back of the book. If
the alphabet is backwards, so are the books!

The direction in which an alphabet is written is simply a
matter of convention. Whether an alphabet is written in one
direction or another does not impact the use of the alphabet
or the meaning of the words. In fact, when the alphabet was
still young, the direction was not firmly established. Some
ancient inscriptions alternate the direction of writing
between left to right and right to left. This type of writing is
called *boustrophedon*, a Greek word meaning "as the ox
turns" when ploughing a field, back-and-forth, in alternating
rows. Just remember, English is written in one direction and
Hebrew is written in the other direction.

Fourth, in the English alphabet, some letters sound alike
and other letters have more than one sound. As adults we
rarely encounter problems with this reality unless we are
trying to pronounce or learn a new word. If you have ever
watched children learn to read, this problem is more appar-
ent. For example, the *c* in "cat" and the *k* in "kite" sound
identical, but *c* and *k* are two different letters. Complicating

this reality is the fact that *c* can sound like the *c* in "cat" but it can also sound like the *c* in "celery." The *f* in "fun" and the *ph* in "phone" sound the same, but they are different symbols. Notice how the *g* in "great" and the *g* in "giant" sound different but they are the same symbol. When you begin to study the Hebrew alphabet, you will notice that some letters represent more than one sound (*BBH* 1.5) and some sounds are represented by more than one letter. Additionally, some letters will look alike, as do the English *b* and *d* (*BBH* 1.7). In time, these alphabetic idiosyncrasies will become inconsequential. In the beginning, however, they can be a pain in the *boustrophedon*.

Without a doubt, the English and Hebrew alphabets, though stemming from a common technological ancestor, do have their differences, and these differences can make learning the Hebrew alphabet a challenge. But there are also numerous similarities between these two alphabets. When possible, focus on the similarities and how certain features correspond. Build as many bridges between these two alphabets as possible, and travel often on those bridges. In this way, you may just become a resident alien in that land across the bridge.

EXERCISES

1. Write out, in order, the twenty-six letters of the English alphabet.

2. Circle the five English vowels.

3. Identify some of the English letters that have similar sounds, like the English letters *k* and *c*.

4. Identify the English letters that have more than one sound, like the English letter *c*.

5. Once you have leaned the Hebrew alphabet, identify where the order of the English and Hebrew letters corresponds and where the order differs.

VOWELS:
Time to Check the Oil!

INTRODUCTION

Imagine what would happen if you were to drive your car without any motor oil? Soon, the car would overheat, the engine would seize, and the motor would be ruined. For a car engine to work properly, it requires a certain amount of oil to lubricate all of the parts, reduce friction, and run smoothly.

Vowels are the motor oil for any spoken language. They lubricate the consonants so that they do not overheat in your mouth. Think about it. When consonants are pronounced, it requires that you close part of your mouth or throat and force air through that restriction. Vowels, on the other hard, are produced in your mouth without any restriction of air flow. So vowels help all of the consonants work together in a smooth and orderly fashion. Without vowels, all of the consonants would crash together in your mouth, creating a huge mess.

Below I have provided an English translation of Psalm 1:1 (NIV) without vowels. Just for fun, try reading the text as written, without pronouncing any vowels. You will quickly understand the impossibility of meaningful pronunciation without vowels.

Pslm 1:1

Blssd s th mn
wh ds nt wlk n th cnsl f th wckd
r stnd n th wy f snnrs
r st n th st f mckrs.

Whew! Take a quick break. You may need a drink of water before you continue any further.

ENGLISH VOWELS

In the English alphabet, there are five vowels: a, e, i, o, and u. Each of these vowels is capable of indicating a variety of different but related sounds depending on the consonantal context in which it occurs. For example, the *a* sound in "fate" is long, but the *a* sound in "fat" is short. The *a* sound in "amuse" is shorter than short, or supershort, almost indistinguishable as an *a*-class vowel.

Sometimes, two vowels will work together in order to create a new vowel sound. Vowel combinations of this type are called "diphthongs." The definition of a diphthong is simple: two vowels that work together as a single vowel. For example, the "ei" in "either" is a diphthong and the "ou" in "bought" is another diphthong. Another one is the "ai" in "aisle." In each case, the "ei," "ou,"and "ai" vowel combinations work together as a single vowel sound. If you ask me, the word "diphthong" is just plain weird!

In English, a vowel can be silent too. For example, the *e* vowels in "fate," "mote," and "bike" are all silent. Each of these words are pronounced without any final *e* sound. As you probably already know, the final *e* vowel marks the previous vowel in each word as long.

In addition to the five standard vowels (a, e, i, o, u), English also has one semivowel – the letter *y*. Notice how the letter *y* functions as a vowel in the following words: "gypsy," "crazy," "syllabus," and "gym." Sometimes, the *y* marks a short vowel, as in "gym." Othertimes, the *y* marks a long vowel, as in "crazy." What makes the letter *y* a semivowel is the fact that it can also function as a consonant, as in "yellow," "yikes," and "canyon."

Finally, it will be helpful to note that English vowels can change within a word, but the consonants are much more stable. For example, notice how the vowels change in the verbs "ring," "rang," and "rung." Vowels can also change in nouns, as in "man" and "men." In both sets of examples, the consonants remain the same, but the vowels change. Such vowel changes indicate modifications in the meaning or the function of the words. In the examples with the verbs (ring, rang, rung), the vowel changes indicate a change in verbal tense (present, past, perfect). In the examples with the nouns (man, men), the vowel changes indicate a change in grammatical number, singular versus plural.

Now remember, the information presented just above is not new information. Everything we have discussed you already know at the intuitive level as a native English speaker (if you are a native English speaker). I have simply taken what you already know and identified appropriate categories and labels. These categories and labels will help to connect *your* English to *God's* Hebrew.

HEBREW VOWELS

In spite of appearances, the English and Hebrew vowel systems share many things in common. Let's take a look.

1. **Vowel Class.** Both English and Hebrew vowels are divided into five vowel classes (a, e, i, o, u). See *BBH* 2.14.1 (but also *BBH* 2.16).

2. **Vowel Length.** Both English and Hebrew vowels can be long, short, or supershort. Supershort vowels are called "reduced" or "Hateph" vowels in Hebrew (*BBH* 2.14.1).

3. **Diphthongs.** Both English and Hebrew have vowel combinations called diphthongs (*BBH* 3.10).

4. **Semi-Vowels.** Like the English letter *y*, there are three Hebrew letters (ה , ו, and י) that can be used either as a consonant or as a vowel. When one of these Hebrew letters is used as a vowel, it is called a "vowel letter" (*BBH* 2.7 and 2.14.2).

5. **Vowel Changes.** Like English vowels, Hebrew vowels can change. Now, this may be the understatement of the chapter. Hebrew vowels change much more frequently and for many more reasons than do English vowels. Just remember, vowels like to change, but consonants are more stable, resisting change.

Once you get to know them, the Hebrew vowels will become quick friends. Why? Because, for the most part, a single Hebrew vowel symbol has a single pronunciation value. In English, a single vowel symbol like "a" can be long, short, or supershort. If you don't know all the rules, and then all of the exceptions, the accurate pronunciation of new or unknown words can be difficult. In Hebrew, however, a single vowel symbol has only one basic pronunciation value. This means that there are three different *a*-class vowel symbols in Hebrew, each with its own unique sound. In general, what you see is what you get when it comes to the pronunciation of biblical Hebrew consonants and vowels. It is more like the stable pronunciation system of the German language than the wacky world of English pronunciation.

There is just one final but important point to make about the Hebrew vowel system. Believe it or not, the vowel system now used for reading biblical Hebrew is not original to the authors of the Hebrew Bible. In fact, when the Hebrew Bible was first written, no vowel symbols were used. The text was purely consonantal! Just like the representation of Psalm 1:1 above, the Hebrew Bible as the biblical authors wrote it contains no written system of vowels. Take a look at Psalm 1:1 one more time.

Pslm 1:1
Blssd s th mn
wh ds nt wlk n th cnsl f th wckd
r stnd n th wy f snnrs
r st n th st f mckrs.

In order to properly read the text as presented above, you would need to provide the English vowels from memory. Yikes! Of course, the vowels always existed in the spoken form of the language. They simply were not represented in writing. That's how it was done, even during the time of Jesus. If you look at any of the Dead Sea Scrolls, you will see that there are no vowel symbols present in the text. It wasn't until the second half of the first millennium A.D. (about 500 years after Christ!) that a group of scribes called the Masoretes created a written system of vowels in order to faithfully record the proper pronunciation of the sacred text (*BBH* 2.1). If you search the Internet, you can easily find photos of the Dead Sea Scrolls and see Hebrew texts without written vowels. You can also view excellent photos of the Aleppo codex online (http://aleppocodex.org/), one of the earliest and best preserved Hebrew manuscripts from the Masoretes. This text has full vowel representation.

It is interesting to note that, in Israel today, only young, elementary-age children read Hebrew texts with written vowels. Adults and other fluent readers continue to read Hebrew without a written vowel system present in the text. The vowels continue to be provided from memory.

EXERCISES

1. List the five vowel classes and the three basic vowel lengths.

2. Define a diphthong.

3. Identify the *a*-class vowels in the following words as long, short, or supershort: America, ant, alumni, ape, female, cast, cake, ran, fable, relate.

4. Identify the *o*-class vowels in the following words as long, short, or supershort: choke, donut, pole, commit, police, portal, mop, wrote, smoke, pot.

5. Circle the diphthongs in the following English words: oil, aisle, fought, receive, relieve, boat, throat, toil, maize, priest.

6. Identify the letter *y* as a consonant or as a vowel in the following English words: backyard, gym, silly, yellow, canyon, yikes, yackety-yak, yappy, burly, royal.

NOUNS:
Name It, and Claim It!

BUILDING BLOCKS

Have you ever observed young children learning how to talk? If so, you may have noticed that nouns are the first things learned, such as "mommy," "daddy," "ball," or "dog." When it comes to language, children learn how to make sense of their new world first by learning the names for those things that are important to them.

A noun is the name given to a person, place, thing, or idea. Nouns can be **concrete**, like the noun "rock," or **abstract**, like the noun "love." Nouns may also be categorized as **common**, like the noun "professor," or **proper**, like the noun "Max." In most languages, including English and Hebrew, nouns are the basic building blocks of the sentence.

Nouns tell us who did what to whom. They come in

many different shapes and sizes, and they are capable of performing a variety of functions.

ENGLISH NOUN QUALITIES

You may be surprised to learn that, in English, nouns have **gender**. A noun can be **masculine, feminine,** or **neuter**. Masculine nouns refer to things that are male. Feminine nouns refer to things that are female. And, finally, neuter nouns refer to things that are not male or female. For example, the nouns "man," "boy," "bull," and "stallion" are masculine and may be referred to with the masculine pronoun "he." The nouns "woman," "girl," "cow," and "mare" are feminine and may be referred to with the feminine pronoun "she." Lastly, the nouns "tree," "book," "pen," and "clock" are neuter and may be referred to with the neuter pronoun "it."

In English, **natural gender** and **grammatical gender** normally correspond. In other words, those nouns that are "naturally" masculine or feminine are usually "grammatically" masculine or feminine.

Masculine (he)	Feminine (she)	Neuter (it)
man	woman	tree
boy	girl	book
bull	cow	pen
stallion	mare	clock

In addition to gender, English nouns also have **number**. They can be **singular** or **plural**. Singular nouns refer to one item and plural nouns refer to more than one item. For example, the singular noun "book" refers to one book but the plural noun "books" refers to more than one book. In addition to singular and plural nouns, English also has something called a **collective** noun. This is a noun that is singular in number but refers to more than one thing, usually something like a group of individuals. Examples of collective nouns include "people," "team," "family," "group," and "class." These nouns are singular in number but refer to more than one person as a single entity.

In English, there are a number of different ways to make a singular noun into a plural noun. Perhaps the most common way is to add the letter *s* to the singular noun. So the singular noun "dog" is made plural by adding *s* (dogs). There are additional ways to pluralize nouns. Some nouns require the addition of *es* (boxes) or *en* (oxen), and others require the modification of vowels within the word. For example, the plural of "tooth" is "teeth." Other nouns may alter their stem as in "children," the plural form of "child." There are other patterns of noun pluralization in English, but this small sample demonstrates the variety of ways in which words can be formed. An awareness of this variety in English will help when you are introduced to the variety of patterns for noun pluralization in Hebrew (*BBH* 4.8).

Singular Noun	Plural Noun	Type of Change
dog	dogs	add **s**
box	boxes	add **es**
ox	oxen	add **en**
tooth	teeth	vowel change
child	children	stem change

ENGLISH NOUN FUNCTIONS

You now know a little about English nouns in terms of their gender (masculine, feminine, and neuter) and number (singular and plural). It is also helpful to consider a few of the ways in which these nouns function. English nouns generally function in one of three ways: subjective, objective, and possessive.

A **subjective noun** is subjective because it functions as the subject of a verbal sentence. In the sentence, "Madie rides a bike," "Madie" is the subject of the sentence because she is performing the verbal action. She "rides" the bike. Subjective nouns can also function as the predicate nominative. A **predicate nominative** is a noun that comes after a form of the verb "to be" and makes an assertion about the subject of the clause. For example, in the expression, "Madie is a child," the proper noun "Madie" is the subject and the common noun "child" is the predicate nominative.

Objective nouns, on the other hand, function as objects. In a sentence, objective nouns may function as direct objects, indirect objects, and the objects of prepositional phrases. Do you see the pattern? They key word is "object." In the sentence, "Madie hit the ball to Max in the backyard," the noun "ball" is the direct object, "Max" is the indirect object, and "backyard" is the object of the preposition "in." Direct and indirect objects participate in a sentence by receiving (directly and indirectly) the verbal action. Prepositional objects follow a preposition. It is really that easy!

Finally, you may be shocked to discover that **possessive nouns** are employed to show possession or ownership. The more common way to indicate possession in English is to add 's to the possessive noun as in "Kacie's Bible" or "the dog's bone." With these examples, "Kacie" and "dog" are made possessive with the addition of 's. Another way to indicate possession in English is to employ the key word "of." Instead of "Kacie's Bible" I could have written "the Bible of Kacie." Similarly, "the dog's bone" could have been written "the bone of the dog." "Of Kacie" and "of the dog" are possessive constructions. Later you will learn that Hebrew uses the "of" construction (*BBH* 10) and not the 's construction in the formation of possessive nouns.

HEBREW NOUNS

English and Hebrew nouns share many things in common. Like English, Hebrew nouns have gender. In terms of gender, Hebrew nouns are masculine or feminine. Hebrew, however, does not have a neuter class of noun. Rather, some Hebrew nouns are labeled as "common," meaning either masculine or feminine.

Another slight difference in terms of gender is the whole notion of *grammatical* verses *natural* gender. English follows natural gender, meaning that the noun "boy" is masculine, the noun "girl" is feminine, and the noun "book" is neuter. In Hebrew, however, nouns are either masculine or feminine, never neuter. For this reason, Hebrew does not always follow what we understand as natural gender. For example, the Hebrew noun תּוֹרָה or "Torah," meaning "law," is feminine, but this does not mean that the concept of "law" is feminine. In Hebrew, this noun simply follows feminine patterns of spelling according to grammatical gender. In English, however, the concept of law is neuter according to what we know as natural gender. Try thinking about it this way— grammatical gender pertains to patterns in spelling or word formation, and natural gender is related to the concepts of male and female (or neither as is the case with neuter).

Connecting the dots between grammatical and natural gender in translation can be confusing at first. In time, however, this concept will become a normal part of your grammatical worldview.

In addition to gender, Hebrew nouns also have number. Like English, Hebrew nouns can be either singular or plural. But unlike English, Hebrew nouns can also be dual, indicating a plurality of two, as in "two eyes" or "two years." In English we indicate a plurality of two with the number "two." In Hebrew, however, you will learn a special noun ending (affix) for this plural category.

EXERCISES

In the following English sentences, nouns are italicized for ease of identification. Label each italicized noun for gender (masculine, feminine, neuter), number (singular, plural), and function (subjective, objective, possessive).

1. In the *beginning, God* created *heaven* and *earth.*

2. *Boaz* met *Ruth* in the *field.*

3. The LORD brought the *Israelites* out of *Egypt.*

4. *Saul* searched the *land* for his *father's donkeys.*

5. *Deborah* battled the *Canaanites* with *Barak.*

6. *Samson's hair* was cut with the *help* of *Delilah.*

7. The *boys* mocked the *prophet's baldness* and so two *she-bears* mauled them.

8. *Jephthah's daughter* mourned the *vow* of her *father.*

9. A *king* will sit on the *throne* of *David* for *eternity.*

10. *Daniel* and *Esther* are *examples* of *faith* during the *exile.*

THE, AND, OF:
Are You Kidding Me?

SMALL WORDS WITH BIG STATUS

You may think that it is absurd to dedicate a whole chapter to a few little words like "the," "and," and "of." However, these three words appear more than any other words in the English Bible.[1] In the NIV translation, for example, the word "the" appears almost 52,000 times; the word "and" appears over 28,000 times; and the word "of" appears over 25,000 times. Together, these three words constitute about fourteen percent of the total words appearing in the average English Bible translation. I'm not kidding!

---

1. The actual numbers vary depending upon the particular translation. For this study, we consulted and searched the NIV, ESV, and NAS95 translations using Accordance for the Mac.

How about a few more amazing statistics? In the English Bible, instances of the words "the," "and," and "of" total approximately 105,000; but the total word count for the Greek New Testament is only about 138,000. In fact, the Hebrew words for "and" and "the" occur more than 75,000 times in the Hebrew Bible, a number well over half of the total word count for the Greek New Testament. In terms of frequency and distribution, therefore, these words are big-time players in the world of the English Bible. They are everywhere, occurring in almost every book, chapter, and verse.

"THE" DEFINITE ARTICLE

The English word "the" is called the **definite article**. It is a little word used to particularize a noun. It changes a noun with indefinite status into a noun with definite status. So, for example, the construction "book" or "a book" is indefinite and nonspecific. With the addition of the definite article, however, that which was once indefinite becomes definite. The indefinite "book" becomes a particular or specific book, "*the* book."

In addition to the definite article, English also has an **indefinite article**; "a" before words beginning with consonants, and "an" before words beginning with a vowel. For example, the constructions "*an* apple" and "*a* banana" are indefinite constructions. "*The* apple" and "*the* banana" are the definite constructions.

In Hebrew, there is no indefinite article. A Hebrew word's indefinite status is simply determined by its lack of definite status.[2] Another slight difference between English

---

2.   A Hebrew noun is considered definite under four conditions:
(1) it appears with a definite article; (2) it appears with a
pronominal suffix; (3) it is a proper name; or (4) it is in construct
with (or bound to) another word that is definite.

and Hebrew is the basic form of the article. In English, the article appears as its own word, "the." In Hebrew, however, the definite article never appears independently as its own word. Rather, it is prefixed to the word that it particularizes. In English, this would look something like "*the*mountain," without any space between the article and the noun. In Hebrew, the prefixed definite article is *ha* and the word for "mountain" is *har*. Therefore, the construction "the mountain" in Hebrew would be something like *ha*har, written and pronounced as a single word (*BBH* 5.2).

AND: KING OF CONJUNCTIONS

Conjunctions are words used to join other words, phrases, and clauses within a sentence. There is a wide variety of conjunctions in the English language. Examples include and, but, or, so, for, and yet. In Hebrew, there are fewer conjunctions. In both languages, however, the conjunction "and" reigns as the king of conjunctions, in terms of both general distribution and breadth of use.

The conjunction "and" may be used to join words, such as "day *and* night" or "good *and* evil." This same conjunction can also join phrases. Examples include "in the morning and in the evening" and "before school *and* after school." In addition to words and phrases, the conjunction "and" is also used to join clauses, as in "Jacob loved Rachel *and* he hated Leah." Simply put, the conjunction "and" is powerful grammatical glue.

The Hebrew word for "and" is the most common word in the Hebrew Bible, appearing over 50,000 times. In terms of basic usage, the Hebrew and English conjunctions function similarly, though there are some special uses in Hebrew that you will study later. In terms of form, the Hebrew conjunction does not appear as its own word. Rather, like the

Hebrew definite article, it is prefixed to other words. So, for example, the English construction "good and evil" would look something like "good ^{and}evil" in Hebrew, with no space between "and" and "evil" (*BBH* 5.7). This phenomenon of prefixing words to other words is common in Hebrew. It will quickly become second nature as you progress in your study of the language.

OF: THE INVISIBLE WORD

If you are the type of a person who needs a label for everything, then the English word "of" would be a preposition. But the label "preposition" simply does not do justice to the variety and diversity of nuances that this little word is capable of depicting.

The English word "of" can express **possession**, as in "the word *of* God"; **origin**, as in "David *of* Bethlehem"; **material**, as in "bricks *of* mud"; and many, many other descriptive nuances. Just look up this word in a standard English dictionary and you will be shocked to see the length of the entry.

For such an important word as this, it is often surprising to discover that there is no word for "of" in biblical Hebrew. You can search high and low, but you will never find any such entry in a Hebrew dictionary (or lexicon). Now, if this is true, then how do you explain the approximately 25,000 occurrences of the word "of" in English translations of the Hebrew Bible? Is it really the invisible word? The answer to this question is the **Hebrew construct state**. Hebrew expresses the "of" relationship between words not with vocabulary, but with syntax, or a special grammatical relationship between words. Let's say, for example, that we wanted to write about a "field of wheat" in Hebrew. To do this, we would simply place the two nouns together, side by side, looking something like "field-wheat" in English. In Hebrew, these two nouns would be bound together, in what is called a "construct chain." Hebrew nouns appearing together in a construct chain require the "of" translation in English. We don't say, "field-wheat." Rather, we say, "field *of* wheat." In English, we need to add "of" for it to make sense. This is just one of those grammatical areas where there is very little correspondence between Hebrew and English. But don't worry, we have dedicated an entire chapter to the Hebrew construct chain in the grammar (*BBH* 10). In time, the foreign will become familiar.

EXERCISES

Due to the nature of the material contained in this chapter, the exercises are slightly different from those appearing in other chapters. That's okay, variety can be a good thing.

1. If you are still not convinced about the pervasive nature of the English words "the," "and," and "of," then read back through this chapter and circle or highlight every time one of these words appears in the text. You might just be surprised.

2. Look up the the English words "the," "and," and "of" in one of the larger standard English dictionaries. You'll know that you have the right dictionary if you need help lifting it off the shelf. Read through the entire entry for each word and outline the variety of nuances each word is capable of communicating. This exercise will really pay off later as you encounter a similar variety in the context of the Hebrew Bible.

PREPOSITIONS:
Watch Where You Sit

INTRODUCTION

During my seminary days, I worked as the secretary for the church that we attended. One of my secretarial responsibilities included the production of the weekly church bulletin. In this bulletin, the Apostles' Creed regularly appeared for recitation during the Sunday worship service. There was one line in this creed that always troubled me; not from a theological perspective, but rather from a grammatical perspective. In the part of the creed that reads, "He ascended into heaven, and sitteth *on* the right hand of God the Father Almighty," the preposition "on" simply did not make sense to me. Was Jesus sitting, physically, "on" God's right hand? I determined that the use of the preposition "on" in this context must be a mistake and proceeded to change "on" to "at" in the bulletin. Well, you can imagine my surprise when the pastor asked me to change "at" back to "on" and to refrain from altering church history in the bulletin. In the end, I capitulated, but a humorous smile still creeps across my face when we read that Jesus sits "on" the Father's right hand. The moral of the story is this: prepositions can cause trouble, so watch where you sit.

ENGLISH PREPOSITIONS

Prepositions are those small, little words in a sentence that describe relationships between other words. In elementary school, you may have learned prepositions with the help of the apple and the worm. The worm crawled *through* the apple. The worm crawled *over* the apple. The worm crawled *under* the apple. The different relationships between the worm and the apple are described with prepositions.

Prepositions introduce **prepositional phrases**. These phrases consist of the preposition, the object of the preposition, and any modifiers of that object. Examples of simple prepositional phrases include *"during* the night," *"on* my desk," *"over* the hill," and *"in front of* the class." The prepositions appear in *italics* and the objects are everything else in the phrase.

Prepositional phrases modify words in a sentence, usually a noun or a verb. When a prepositional phrase modifies a noun, it is **adjectival**. This means that it functions like an adjective. In the sentence, "the woman *with green eyes* is my wife," the prepositional phrase "with green eyes" modifies the noun "woman" and so this prepositional phrase is adjectival.

When a prepositional phrase modifies a verb, it is **adverbial**. This means that it functions like an adverb. In the sentence, "I love my wife *with all of my heart*," the prepositional phrase "with all of my heart" modifies the verb "love," and so this prepositional phrase is adverbial.

In terms of form, it is helpful to note that most prepositions consist of a single word, such as "to," "for," "in," "at," "against," "by," or "as." Some English prepositions, however, consist of more than one word. Examples include "according to," "in front of," "because of," and "in place of."

HEBREW PREPOSITIONS

In terms of basic grammar, English and Hebrew prepositions are identical. In Hebrew, **prepositions** introduce prepositional phrases. The Hebrew **prepositional phrase** consists of the preposition, the object of the preposition, and any modifiers of that object. As in English, these Hebrew prepositional phrases modify both verbs and nouns. As such, they function either **adjectivally** (modifying nouns) or **adverbially** (modifying verbs).

Like English, Hebrew prepositions come in a number of different forms. Some Hebrew prepositions consist of a single word. These are **independent** prepositions (*BBH* 6.2). Other Hebrew prepositions are formed with more than one word. These are known as **compound** prepositions (*BBH* 6.11). Independent and compound Hebrew prepositions are similar in formation to English prepositions.

In terms of form, there is one category of Hebrew preposition that is not like English. Prepositions of this sort are called **inseparable** prepositions (*BBH* 6.4). These prepositions are attached directly to their object – something like a prefix. For example, the English construction "in God" appears in Hebrew as something like "[in]God." Notice how there is no space between the preposition "in" and its object, "God." Don't worry, though. There are only three (and one half) inseparable prepositions in Hebrew. In fact, there are altogether fewer prepositions in Hebrew than there are in English. In English, there are over one hundred different prepositions. In Hebrew, however, there are only about thirty prepositions to learn. This is the good news of Hebrew prepositions!

EXERCISES

In the following exercises, prepositional phrases appear in italics. Circle the preposition, underline the object of the preposition, and draw a line from the prepositional phrase to the word it modifies.

1.   *In the beginning* God created the heavens and the earth.

2.   The Spirit of God was hovering *over the waters*.

3.   So God created man *in his own image, in the image of God* he created him;

4.   Blessed is the man who does not walk *in the counsel of the wicked* or stand *in the way of sinners* or sit *in the seat of mockers*.

5.   The LORD has sought out a man *after his own heart*.

6.   The Philistines occupied one hill and the Israelites another, with the valley *between them*.

7.   Early *in the morning* David left the flock with a shepherd, loaded up and set out, as Jesse had directed.

8.   Did God really say, "You must not eat from any tree *in the garden?*"

9.   And they hid from the LORD God *among the trees of the garden*.

10. And I will put enmity *between you and the woman*, and *between your offspring and hers*.

ADJECTIVES:
Our Theology Requires Modification

INTRODUCTION

Adjectives are the spices of the grammatical world. They add flavor, texture, and color to the banquet of language. It would be difficult to think about life without adjectives. We might be tempted to think of such a life as bland, dull, or dreary. However, this would be impossible because "bland," "dull," and "dreary" are adjectives. No, our lives could be neither "good," "bad," nor "mediocre." These are also adjectives.

Just like life, without adjectives our knowledge of God would be seriously impoverished. Much of what we know about God's attributes from the Old Testament comes to us through adjectives. We learn that God is "compassionate," "gracious," and "patient" (Exodus 34:6). He is "wonderful,"

"mighty," and "everlasting" (Isaiah 9:6). He is the "first" and
the "last" (Isaiah 44:6). And these are just three verses. Other
adjectives in the Old Testament teach us that God is "righteous" (Psalm 11:7), "good" and "upright" (Psalm 25:8),
"strong" and "mighty" (Psalm 24:8), "most high" (Genesis
14:22), "glorious" (Exodus 15:11), "near" (Psalm 145:18), and
three-times "holy" (Isaiah 6:3). Adjectives are modifiers, and
our theology requires modification!

ENGLISH ADJECTIVES

Adjectives are modifiers. They "modify, describe, characterize, or classify nouns" (*BBH* 7.1). Some grammars will
describe adjectives as those words that place restrictions on
nouns. For example, in a phrase like "the *good* book," the
adjective "good" describes the book in a way that restricts
our identification of the book as one that is good. In other
words, adjectives build fences around nouns in order to pro-
tect their identity. Adjectival usage falls into three basic categories: attributive, predicative, and substantive. In the first
two categories, the adjective modifies a noun. In the substantive category, the adjective functions like a noun.

In English, the **attributive adjective** is placed directly
before the noun it modifies. In the following examples, the
attributive adjectives appear directly in front of the nouns
that they modify.

beautiful woman	upright man
false prophet	righteous king
holy smoke	wise judge

If the noun being modified is definite or indefinite, the
definite or indefinite article is placed before the adjective,
not before the noun, as the following examples illustrate
(remember that Hebrew does not have an indefinite article).

the beautiful woman	an upright man
the false prophet	a righteous king
the holy smoke	a wise judge

In English, the **predicative adjective** also modifies a noun, but in a way different than the attributive adjective. Predicate adjectives modify nouns with the help of the verb "to be." In this usage, the noun or subject is connected to the adjective or predicate by a form of the verb "to be" (or another linking verb). You should also note that, in this case, the noun comes first and the adjective comes after the verb "to be," as the following examples illustrate.

the woman was beautiful	a man is upright
the prophet was false	a king is righteous
the smoke was holy	a judge is wise

In English, the **substantive adjective** does not modify a noun, but functions as a noun. In an example like, "*Red* is my favorite color," the adjective "red" does not modify another noun but rather functions like a noun. In this case, the adjective "red" is the subject of the sentence. In the example, "Our budget operates in the *red*," the adjective "red" again does not modify another noun. Rather, the adjective "red" functions as the object of the preposition "in."

Finally, we should note that the form of the English adjective is stable. This means that its form is not affected by the type of noun it modifies in the categories of gender and number. For example, the adjective "good" can modify "man" (masculine), "woman" (feminine), or "book" (neuter) without any change in form. What is true for gender is also true for number. The same adjective "good" can also modify the plural nouns "men," "women," and "books" without any change in form. In this case, what is true for English is *not* true for Hebrew.

HEBREW ADJECTIVES

In terms of basic function, Hebrew adjectives function much like English adjectives (*BBH* 7.4). In the attributive and predicative categories of usage, however, the way in which the Hebrew nouns and adjectives appear together is somewhat different.

With the attributive usage, the English construction "the wise prophet" appears in Hebrew as "the prophet the wise." The basic constructions differ in arrangement, but the meaning in the same. In English, the definite article appears once, and the adjective comes before the noun. In Hebrew, however, the definite article appears twice, and the noun comes before the adjective.

Similarly, the way in which English and Hebrew construct sentences using predicate adjectives also differs. For example, the English construction, "the prophet is wise" could appear in Hebrew as either "the prophet wise" or "wise the prophet." There are two things to take note of with this example. First, the predicate adjective can come before or after the noun, and it never takes the definite article. Second, there is no form of the verb "to be." It is simply implied by the Hebrew construction itself, and so it must be added to the English translation. In Hebrew, this is called a **verbless clause** because there is *no verb in the clause*. Imagine that!

Finally, we noted above that the form of the English adjective is stable. It does not change depending on the type of noun it modifies. The English adjective is rock solid. It is made from granite. In Hebrew, however, the form of the adjective changes to match the form of the noun in the categories of gender and number. So, an expression in English like "the great kings" would need to be written in Hebrew as something like "the kings the greats." Now, in English, a construction of this type is impossible. But you get the point. In Hebrew, a noun with plural endings requires an adjective with plural endings. Similarly, nouns with feminine endings would require adjectives with feminine endings. Hebrew adjectives are like chameleons, they like to blend in to their environment.

You are now beginning to observe that, when translating Hebrew into English, you will not always want to follow the word order of the Hebrew construction. To do so would often result in bad, or even unintelligible, English. When working to translate a foreign language like Hebrew, you must learn to translate both the foreign words and the foreign grammar. Otherwise, you might begin to think that your Bible was written by someone like Yoda. Good, this would not be, hmm!

EXERCISES

In the following exercises, adjectives appear in italics. In each case, identify the use of the English adjective as either attributive, predicative, or substantive.

1. God saw that the light was *good*.

2. God made two *great* lights—the *greater* light to govern the day and the *lesser* light to govern the night.

3. You must not eat from the tree of the knowledge of *good* and *evil*, for when you eat of it you will surely die.

4. The man and his wife were *naked*, and they felt no shame.

5. Take with you *seven* of every kind of *clean* animal, a male and its mate, and *two* of every kind of *unclean* animal, a male and its mate.

6. Now Sarai was *barren*; she had no children.

7. Now there was a famine in the land, and Abram
    went down to Egypt to live there for a while because
    the famine was *severe*.

8. Now the men of Sodom were very *wicked* and *sinful*
    to the LORD.

9. May they be blotted out of the book of life and not
    be listed with the *righteous*.

10. Yet I am *poor* and *needy*; come quickly to me, O God.

PRONOUNS:
Grammatical Stunt Doubles

INTRODUCTION

Pronouns are the substitute teachers, surrogate mothers, pinch hitters, union scabs, and stunt doubles of the grammatical world. What do these types of people have in common? The answer is that they replace other people. Pronouns do the same thing, but they replace nouns.

The pronoun system is basic. There are really only two parts to it: (1) the pronoun and (2) its antecedent. The **pronoun** is the substitute and the **antecedent** is what was substituted. So, in the example, "Moses struck the rock; *he* hit *it* with the staff," there are two different pronouns with two different antecedents.

The first pronoun is "he" and it takes the place of "Moses." Another way to say this is that the antecedent of "he" is "Moses." In English, we know that "Moses" and "he" go together because they are both singular and masculine. In other words, they match.

The second pronoun in our example is "it" and it takes the place of "rock." The antecedent of "it" is "rock." Once again, we know that "rock" and "it" go together because they are both singular and neuter. Again, note that the pronoun and its antecedent match in gender and number.

In both English and Hebrew, there are several different types of pronouns. For the purposes of studying Hebrew, we will take a look at four different types of English pronouns: personal, demonstrative, relative, and interrogative.

PERSONAL PRONOUNS

Personal pronouns are the most common type of pronoun and, because of this, they are also the most irregular or varied in terms of form. Remember this grammatical principle; it will serve you well: *that which is most common is also most irregular*. Think, for example, of the English verb "to be." It is the most common English verb and so, correspondingly, exhibits the greatest diversity in form: am, is, are, was, were, be, being, and been.

English personal pronouns come in a variety of forms. These pronouns are like golf clubs. The shape of the club is determined by a number of different factors, including its function, the size of the golfer, the strength of the golfer, and whether the golfer is right or left handed. For example, the driver is used to achieve distance, the pitching wedge for height, and the putter for accuracy. The form of each club is determined by its function and its function determines form.

In English, the form of the personal pronoun is determined by as many as four different factors: function, person, gender, and number. Pronouns function like nouns, so they may be either subjective, objective, or possessive. They also encode gender and number. In addition to masculine, feminine, and neuter pronouns (in the third person), there is also a "common" category of gender (in the first and second person). A pronoun with **common gender** can refer to both men and women at the same time, such as "us" or "you." For a review of these noun categories, see chapter 3 in this book.

In addition to function, gender, and number, personal pronouns are also shaped by what is called "person." There are three persons in English: first, second, and third. Grammatical person characterizes the relationship between the speaker and what is being spoken about. In the **first person**, the speaker includes himself or herself. In the **second person**, the speaker is addressing another person or group of people. Lastly, the **third person** is indirect or distant. In other words, the speaker and the thing being spoken about are not engaged or part of the same context. The chart below summarizes all of this pronominal chaos. Remember, you already know intuitively how this stuff works. We are simply providing labels and categories that will aid your study of foreign languages, especially Hebrew (see *BBH* 8.3).

Person	Subjective	Objective	Possessive
1st Singular	I	me	my, mine
1st Plural	we	us	our, ours
2nd Singular	you	you	your, yours
2nd Plural	you	you	your, yours
3rd Singular	he/she/it	him/her/it	his/hers/its
3rd Plural	they	them	theirs

Hebrew pronouns are remarkably similar to English pronouns. In Hebrew, the personal pronouns are shaped by the same four categories: function, person, gender, and number. In terms of person, there is first, second, and third persons. In the gender category, there are masculine and feminine in the second and third persons, and common in the first person, both singular and plural. Hebrew pronouns also vary depending upon their function, but not in quite the same way as in English.

Hebrew uses two different sets of personal pronouns; one set is for the subjective case and the other set is for the objective and possessive cases. The subjective personal pronouns are called "independent personal pronouns" because they stand alone as "independent" words (*BBH* 8.2–4), just like English pronouns.

The objective and possessive pronouns, on the other hand, are not independent, but rather suffixed. This means that they are attached directly to the end of other words as suffixes (*BBH* 9, 19). For example, the English construction "my God" looks something like "God^my" in Hebrew. In English, the possessive pronoun "my" appears *independently* as its own word *before* the noun. In Hebrew, the possessive pronoun appears attached or *affixed* to the *end* of the noun.

Hebrew uses the same set of pronouns for the objective and possessive categories. The difference is that possessive pronouns are attached as suffixes to nouns, and objective pronouns are attached as suffixes to verbs and prepositions. So, by way of example, the English constructions "kill him" or "by him" looks something like "kill^him" and "by^him" in Hebrew. In Hebrew, the objective pronoun is attached directly to the end of the verb or preposition. It is not independent, meaning that it does not appear separately as its own word in Hebrew. Capiche?

DEMONSTRATIVE PRONOUNS

Didn't your parents ever teach you that its not polite to point? Well, demonstratives are just plain rude. They love to point. In English, the demonstrative pronoun *points* to other nouns. There are two sets. The **near demonstratives** are "this" (singular) and "these" (plural). The **far demonstratives** are "that" (singular) and "those" (plural). The categories of near and far describe the relative proximity between the speaker and the demonstrative's antecedent. "This" is nearer than "that."

One oddity of the demonstrative pronoun is that it can also function as an adjective. In the example, "this is my book," the demonstrative "this" stands alone and functions as the subject of the sentence. In this case, the demonstrative "this" is a pronoun. However, in the example, "that book is mine," the demonstrative "that" modifies the noun "book" and stands together with "book" as the subject of the sentence. In that case, the demonstrative "that" functions as an adjective.

Everything described above for English demonstratives also applies to Hebrew demonstratives (*BBH* 8.5–7). The biggest difference between the two languages is that Hebrew demonstratives are inflected for gender in the singular. This simply means that Hebrew has two different words for "this" and two different words for "that"; one form is for the masculine and the other form is for the feminine. No big deal!

RELATIVE PRONOUNS

Relative pronouns do not deny the possibility of absolute truth. Rather, these pronouns introduce a relative clause, the entirety of which usually modifies a previous noun. The basic relatives in English are "that" plus a number of "wh-" words, including "who," "whom," "whose," "what," and "which."

So how do these things work? To begin with, the relative pronoun connects a descriptive or adjectival clause to a previous noun. The relative pronoun stands for the noun being modified. In the sentence, "the boy *who killed Goliath* became king," the relative clause is "who killed Goliath." The relative pronoun is "who" and it connects the relative clause to the noun "boy." Which "boy"? The one "who killed Goliath."

The English relative clause functions just like the Hebrew relative clause. The main difference between these two systems is the number of relative pronoun options. In English, there are over half a dozen relative pronouns (that, who, whom, whose, what, which). In Hebrew, however, there is only one main relative pronoun and it never changes form (אֲשֶׁר; *BBH* 8.8). So, in terms of vocabulary, learning this pronoun is easy. The difficulty will come in translation. Into which of the six or so English relative pronouns do I translate this single Hebrew pronoun? At this point you could take the advice of some of my students – "just guess" – or you could follow two general guidelines: (1) use "that" for essential information and "which" for nonessential information; and (2) use "what" and "which" to refer to things and "who," "whom," and "whose" to refer to people.[1]

INTERROGATIVE PRONOUNS

Last I checked, interrogative pronouns were in trouble. They were being *questioned* for their role in criminal interro-

---

1.   Robert Perrin, *The Beacon Handbook* (Boston: Houghton Mifflin Company, 1987), 107.

gations. Why? Because interrogative pronouns are used to "interrogate" or ask questions. Some of the English interrogative pronouns are "who," "whom," "what," "which," and "whose." In Hebrew, there are only two main interrogatives, "who" and "what." When God spoke to the woman in Genesis 3, he asked, "What (מָה) is this you have done?" When God spoke to the man in the same chapter, he asked, "Who (מִי) told you that you were naked?" As you can see from these examples, English and Hebrew interrogative pronouns function in the same way. Note, however, that there is no question mark (?) in Hebrew, only in English.

SUMMARY

1. **Personal pronouns** take the place of nouns. The noun that the pronoun replaces is called the antecedent (I, you [singular], he, she, it, we, you [plural], they).

2. **Demonstrative pronouns** point to other nouns. Remember that these can also function as adjectives (this, these, that, those).

3. **Relative pronouns** introduce relative clauses, which modify previous nouns (that, who, whom, which, whose).

4. **Interrogative pronouns** are used to ask questions (who, whom, what, which, and whose).

EXERCISES

In the following exercises, pronouns appear in italics. In each case, identify the the type of English pronoun (personal, demonstrative, relative, or interrogative). If the pronoun is personal, identify its function as subjective, objective, or possessive. If it is demonstrative, identify it as a demonstrative pronoun or demonstrative adjective. If it is a relative pronoun, identify the noun it modifies.

1. *He* answered, "*I* heard *you* in the garden, and *I* was afraid because *I* was naked; so *I* hid."

2. And *he* said, "*Who* told *you* that *you* were naked? Have *you* eaten from the tree *that I* commanded *you* not to eat from?"

3. And *I* will put enmity between *you* and the woman, and between *your* offspring and *hers*; *he* will crush *your* head, and *you* will strike *his* heel.

4. *I* am the LORD your God, *who* brought *you* out of Egypt.

5. *What* is *my* crime? *What* sin have *I* committed for *which you* hunt *me* down? Now that *you* have searched through all *my* goods, *what* have *you* found *that* belongs to *your* household?

6. In God, *whose* word *I* praise, in God *I* trust; *I* will not be afraid. *What* can mortal man do to *me*?

7. *Who* is *he*, *this* King of glory? The LORD Almighty—*he* is the King of glory.

8. *This* is the day the LORD has made; let *us* rejoice and be glad in *it*.

9. *He* brought *them* to the man to see *what he* would name *them*; and *whatever* the man called each living creature, *that* was *its* name.

10. *My* God, *my* God, why have *you* forsaken *me*? Why are *you* so far from saving *me*, so far from the words of *my* groaning?

THE SENTENCE:
Parts Is Parts!

INTRODUCTION

Do you remember the old Wendy's commercial poking fun at the processed chicken of their competitors? There is a good line in that ad, "As I here tell, all the parts are crammed into one big part . . . and parts is parts!" Now, the commercial ad is talking about chicken sandwiches, but you might be feeling the same way about grammar. So far, we have been talking about all of the different grammatical "parts." But how are all these parts "crammed into one big part"? The answer is, "The sentence."

Up to this point, we have been working to understand some of the noun "parts" in a sentence. In the next several chapters, we will turn our attention to the many different verb "parts." Before we make this transition, however, let's pause to consider some of the basic issues related to how all these parts will get "crammed together" into English and Hebrew sentences.

WORDS, PHRASES, AND CLAUSES

In previous chapters, we have used grammatical terms and labels such as "word," "phrase," "clause," and "sentence" without any explanation or definition. It is now time to provide some basic definitions in order to ensure clarity and accuracy.

The definition of a **word** is simple. A word is a word, an assembly of letters into a meaningful unit. For example, "cat" is a word. It is an assembly of three letters into a noun whose reference is well known and commonly understood. On the other hand, something like "gxtqllyefv" is not a word. Sure, it is an assembly of letters, but this particular assembly is not meaningful. It is unknown and has no reference to reality. But you already know that.

A **phrase** is a group of related words that lacks a subject or predicate (or both). The subject is the noun or pronoun that a clause makes a statement about, like the subject of a verb, and a predicate consists of the statement about the subject. So, for example, in the sentence, "David struck down Goliath with sling and stone," "David" is the subject, and everything else is the predicate. A phrase cannot stand alone. It must be connected to something else in a larger grammatical unit that can stand alone, such as an indepen-dent clause. In the example above, "with sling and stone" is a prepositional phrase (see chapter 5), and it would not form a complete thought if it were to appear by itself. It only makes sense in the context of the clause to which it is connected.

Like a phrase, a clause consists of a group of words. But unlike a phrase, a **clause** must have a subject and predicate. The absence or presence of a subject and predicate is what distinguishes a phrase from a clause. Using the same example from above, "David struck down Golliath," the presence of the subject "David" and the predicate "struck down Golliath" creates a clause. This independent clause can stand alone and it forms a complete thought or sentence. It does not require the additional prepositional phrase "with sling and stone" to make sense.

There are two basic clause categories: independent and dependent. Independent clauses are, well, "independent." They are the Marlborough men of the sentence world. They can stand alone or provide the point of contact for those other, less "manly" clauses, the dependent clauses.

By way of contrast, dependent clauses are not independent, but rather depend on their connection to main or independent clauses. One example of a dependent clause is the relative clause. We studied the relative clause in chapter 7. It is usually easy to spot a dependent clause. They normally begin with a key word that makes them subordinate to another clause. Some of these key words in English are that, since, because, who, if, and while.

Compared to languages like English or Greek, Hebrew has relatively few subordinate clauses. In fact, it is fair to say that biblical Hebrew has only two major subordinate clauses – those that begin with אֲשֶׁר (who, that) and those that begin with כִּי (because, since, that). There are a few others, but they are less common (see *BBH* 20.12 and 23.8–9).

Finally, a **sentence** consists of a least one independent clause. This is the minimum. Sentences can contain much, much more. By way of example, a single sentence may contain multiple independent clauses, multiple dependent clauses, numerous phrases, and lots and lots of words.

English sentences range from simple to very complex. In biblical Hebrew, you will be glad to know that there is a preference for simpler sentence constructions.

WORD ORDER

In a sentence, different words have different functions. Some words, for example, may function as the subject of a verb, while others may function as the verbal object. Still other words may have modifying functions. So how is a word's function in a sentence identified?

Different languages identify a word's function within a sentence in different ways. Some languages, like Greek, Latin, and German, use a system of **case endings** to mark word function. In systems like these, the form of the word determines the function of the word in the sentence.

Other languages, like Hebrew, Spanish, and English, use **word order** to indicate word function within a sentence. For example, in the sentence, "Miles loves Laurie," we know that "Miles" is the subject and "Laurie" is the object of the verb because "Miles" comes before the verb and "Laurie" follows the verb. Laurie is the object of Miles's love. However, if we switch the word order to "Laurie loves Miles," "Laurie" is now the subject and "Miles" is the object of the verb. Miles is now the object of Laurie's love. So, when "Miles" comes before the verb, he is the subject of the verb. But, when "Miles" comes after the verb, he is the object of the verb. The form of the word "Miles" stays the same but its position in the sentence changes to indicate a change in function. The issue of word order to determine a word's function within a sentence applies to both English and Hebrew.

In English, the general word order is subject-verb-object-modifier (abbreviated SVOM). This word order is illustrated by the following example: "Ehud sent a message to Eglon with his sword."

Subject:	Ehud
Verb:	sent
Direct Object:	a message
Indirect Object:	to Eglon
Modifier:	with his sword

In the above example, there are two objects: direct and indirect. Direct objects receive the action of the verb and indirect objects identify "to whom" or "for whom" the action is done. In English, the order of direct and indirect objects may vary within a clause. The above example could have been written as, "Ehud sent Eglon a message with his sword." If the indirect object follows the direct object, use of the key word "to" or "for" helps to make sense of the order.

In Hebrew, standard word order is traditionally identified as verb subject object modifier (abbreviated VSOM). The main difference between between English and Hebrew word order, therefore, is the position of the subject with respect to the position of the verb. English prefers the subject-verb (SV) order while Hebrew prefers the verb-subject order (VS).[1] We can illustrate this slight difference by modifying the example above to comply with Hebrew word order, "Sent Ehud Eglon a message with a sword." Of course this seems awkward because of our familiarity with English word order.

Sometimes, there are ways around this confusion. Hebrew can explicitly mark a (definite) direct object by placing the word אֵת just before the direct object. This little word

---

1.   Some Hebrew grammarians argue for SVOM as standard word order in biblical Hebrew. In fact, both SV and VS orders appear with measured frequency in the Hebrew Bible. It may be the case that issues of macro-syntax control the selection of word order.

is not translated. It has absolutely no lexical value. Rather, it simply identifies the following word as the direct object of the verb. In time, this little word will become your friend, helping you find your way out of the maze of Hebrew word order.

In addition to standard word order in sentences, there are other areas where word order differs between English and Hebrew. A few examples below illustrate instances of word order variation in topics previously covered in this book:

English Example	Hebrew Equivalent	Construction
the good king	the king the good	attributive adj
the king is good	good the king/the king good	predicate adj
this king	the king the this	demonstrative adj
this is the king	this the king/the king this	demonstrative pron
this good king	the king the good the this	demonstrative adj with attributive adj
David killed Goliath	killed David Goliath	simple sentence

EXERCISES

Identify the different parts of each sentence with the following labels: subject (s), verb (v), object (o), and modifier (m). The first exercise has been done by way of example. Note that each part is not required in each sentence. Only the subject and verb are required in English.

          m   **s**   **v**   **o**

1. (In the beginning), God created (the heavens).

2. God created man in his image.

3. The Spirit of God hovered over the waters.

4. The land produced vegetation on the third day.

5. God made the wild animals according to their kinds.

6. I give every green plant to man for food.

7. On the seventh day God finished the work.

8. The LORD God had not sent rain upon the earth.

9. I will make a helper for him according to his needs.

10. She was taken out of man.

MOOD, TENSE, ASPECT:
Understanding Verb Psychology

INTRODUCTION

Okay, it is time to turn our attention to the study of the English verb system. With such a study, there is both good news and bad news. The bad news is that the English verb system is large, complicated, and nuanced. The good news is that most of us, as native speakers, are already familiar with the basics, at least intuitively.

Most of this chapter simply consists of attaching some labels to certain basic verbal realities. The purpose of this "labeling" will be to create points of contact between the English and Hebrew verb systems. For example, when working to understand "mood," "tense," or "aspect" in Hebrew, it will help to have a basic concept of how these same realities function in English. At least I hope it will.

Finally, know this: **verbs** are those words in a language used to describe an action or state of being. They are the movers and shakers of the grammatical world. They are the electricity that runs through the sentence, causing the lights to go on as actions and ideas come to life.

MOOD: DON'T CRY!

Verbs have mood, but this does not mean that they are moody. In psychology, mood describes how someone feels – grumpy, sad, happy, etc. We commonly say, "she is in a good mood" or "he was in a bad mood." In grammar, however, the concept of mood describes how a verb relates to reality. In current studies, it is difficult to determine exactly how many different moods exist in the English language. At the very least, there are three basic English moods.

The most common mood in any language is the indicative mood. The **indicative mood** (BBH 13–17, 23) is the mood of factuality. It is used to describe reality or ask questions. For example, sentences like "David *wept*" or "Did David *weep*?" occur in the indicative mood because they either describe reality or attempt to identify reality by way of interrogation.

The second basic English mood is the imperative mood. The **imperative mood** (BBH 18, 23) is bossy and needy. It is the mood of commands and requests. Sentences like "*Honor* your father and mother!" or "Let us *worship* the LORD" are in the imperative mood because these verbs are used, not to describe reality, but to impose the will of the speaker on reality. In other words, this mood is used when the speaker wants to change reality. The imperative mood may also be referred to as **volitional** or **projective**. The label "volitional" emphasizes the focus on the will of the speaker while the label "projective" characterizes the desire of the speaker to "project" his or her will onto reality.

The third basic English mood is the subjunctive mood. The **subjunctive** mood (*BBH* 23.7–9) is the mood of possibility or probability, wishes, opinions, and hypothetical statements. The subjunctive is, in some sense, the opposite of the indicative mood. The indicative mood describes what is intended as real; the subjunctive mood describes what is hypothetical or expected. For example, the sentence, "If Moses had not struck the rock a second time, he would have entered the promised land," describes a hypothetical situation. It never really happened that way.

So, by way of summary, the indicative mood is used to describe or determine reality. The imperative mood is used when the speaker wants to change or shape reality. And, finally, the subjunctive mood is used to describe reality as conditional, hypothetical, or expected. There are a variety of different ways in English to express the different moods, but that is not our concern at this point. What you want to take from this section is that languages use grammatical mood when it comes to the portrayal of reality and there are three basic grammatical moods. These same three moods also exist in Hebrew.

TENSE: RELAX!

So, a man stormed into his doctor's office and blurted out, "I'm a teepee, I'm a wigwam, I'm a teepee, I'm a wigwam." To this the doctor replied, "Relax, you're too tense." Or did he really mean, "two tents"? Either way, this has nothing to do with verbs, but the joke still makes me smile. Thanks, Nina!

No, when is comes to verbs, grammatical tense is not related to the psychological phenomenon of stress or anxiety. Rather, **grammatical tense** describes the time of the verbal action portrayed by the speaker or writer. There are only three such tenses in English. They are the past tense, the present tense, and the future tense. Past actions are described with the **past tense**. Present actions are described with the **present tense**. And, future actions are described with the **future tense**. The examples provided below demonstrate how the same verbal action can be portrayed in three different tenses or time frames.

Elijah *slept* by the river.	**Past Tense**
Elijah *sleeps* by the river.	**Present Tense**
Elijah *will sleep* by the river.	**Future Tense**

Okay, you've got to admit that this is pretty easy. So relax, there is no need to be so tense! What else is there besides the past, present, and future? This just about covers everything. Finally, note that Hebrew verbs can express the same three tenses, just not in the same way as English verbs do (*BBII* 13, 15, 17, and 23.5–6).

ASPECT: THAT'S YOUR PERSPECTIVE.

There is just one more topic to cover in this chapter and then we are done. That topic is verbal aspect. Verbal **aspect** characterizes the way in which a verb portrays its own action. Is the action ongoing? Is it completed? Is it completed with ongoing effects? In English there are as many as four different verbal aspects of this type. They are labelled as simple, perfect, progressive, and perfect progressive.

Think of the **simple aspect** as the default aspect. It communicates very little about the verbal action, simply that it happened (Elijah sleeps). The **perfect aspect** describes an action that occurred in the past, but the impact of that action is still relevant at the time of writing or speaking (Elijah has slept). The **progressive aspect** portrays the verbal action as continuous or ongoing (Elijah is sleeping). And, lastly, the **perfect progressive** aspect portrays the verbal action as continuous or ongoing, but not necessarily at the time of speaking or writing (Elijah has been sleeping). I recognize that this might seem a bit complicated or nuanced, but study the chart below. This chart shows how tense and aspect intersect in the indicative mood. It should help clear things up.

	Simple Aspect	Perfective Aspect	Progressive Aspect	Perfect Progressive
Present Tense	he runs	he has run	he is running	he has been running
Past Tense	he ran	he had run	he was running	he had been running
Future Tense	he will run	he will have run	he will be running	he will have been running

Finally, be encouraged that the Hebrew verb system is not as complicated as the English verb system (though capable of many of the same nuances). In Hebrew, there are only two main verbal aspects, perfective (*BBH* 13.3) and imperfective (*BBH* 15.2).

SUMMARY: MOOD, TENSE, & ASPECT

1. Grammatical **mood** characterizes a verb's portrayal of reality (indicative, imperative, subjunctive).

2. Grammatical **tense** describes the relationship between the time of verbal action and the time of speaking or writing (past, present, future).

3.   Grammatical **aspect** characterizes the way in which a verbs portrays its own action (simple, perfect, progressive, perfect progressive).

EXERCISES

Take a break! There are no exercises for this chapter. I fear that this *aspect* of our discussion has made you *tense* and put you into a bad *mood*.

10

PERSON, GENDER, NUMBER:
Understanding Verb Reference

INTRODUCTION

Fasten your seat belt! We're not done yet. When it comes to verbs, there is so much more wonderful grammatical information that we just couldn't help but write another chapter. In the last chapter, we covered the exciting topics of mood, tense, and aspect as they relate to verbs. Now, in this chapter, we will add to our verbal knowledge the concepts of person, gender, and number.

Really, from a grammatical perspective, what could be more exciting? It's time for the verbal ultrasound. Will it be a girl, a boy, or one of each? However, before we get started, note that the information covered in this chapter, and in chapters 9 and 11, corresponds to realities that span the entire verb system. You may be hunting around in your

Hebrew grammar in order to determine how this chapter might match up to one of the chapters in the Hebrew grammar. Stop looking. There is no such match. The purpose of chapters 9 through 11 in this text is to provide you with a summary framework for the entire verb system. It explains, for example, the necessary background for understanding all of the information presented in chapters 12 through 35 of *Basics of Biblical Hebrew* – or, dare we even mention, any treatment of the Hebrew verb system in one of the many other available Hebrew grammars. So relax, the goal is orientation.

PERSON, GENDER, & NUMBER

Like the pronouns back in chapter 7, verbs have person, gender, and number. By way of example, flip back to the summary chart in chapter 9 (p. 66), which organizes verbs into the categories of tense and aspect (I'll wait while you flip). Note that all of the verbs in this chart appear with the personal pronoun "he," which is third person, masculine, and singular, as in, *"he* ran." Now to be clear, not all verbs have these qualities. Some verb forms simply do not encode person, gender, or number. The participle ("running") and the infinitive ("to run") are two examples. Constructions such as "she running" or "he to run" simply don't work in English. For now, don't worry about these verb forms. We will cover them in subsequent chapters. In this section, we will concern ourselves only with those verb forms that express person, gender, and number (*BBH* 13–18).

Back in the pronoun chapter, we learned that there are three persons (first, second, and third), two numbers (singular and plural), and three genders (masculine, feminine, and neuter – as well as common, meaning masculine and/or feminine). These same realities apply to verbs. In fact,

English verbs use nouns or personal pronouns to indicate person, gender, and number. In most cases, the form of the verb itself does not encode this information.

It is now time for your middle school education to pay off. Did your English grammar teacher ever make you conjugate English verbs? Mine sure did. At the time, I was less than enthusiastic about the exercise. But now, I am thankful. To conjugate a verb is to render that verb into the categories of person, gender, and number. By way of example, the chart below displays the conjugations of the present, past, and future tenses in the simple aspect with the verb "to run."

	Past Tense	Present Tense	Future Tense
1cs	I ran	I run	I will run
2cs	you ran	you run	you will run
3(mfn)s	he, she, it ran	he, she, it runs	he, she, it will run
1cp	we ran	we run	we will run
2cp	you ran	you run	you will run
3cp	they ran	they run	they will run

Notice how, in terms of person, the verbs are arranged in the order of first, second, and third person (1cs, 2cs, 3ms, etc). In terms of number, the first set of three forms is singular (1cs, 2cs, 3[mfn]s), and the second set of three forms is plural (1cp, 2cp, 3[mfn]p).

The issue of gender is a little more complicated. In the first and second person, as well as in the third person plural, the gender category is "common," meaning that those forms of the conjugation can be used for either masculine or feminine subjects. In other words, the pronouns "I," "we," "you," and "they" are used with reference to both men and women. In the third person singular, however, the indication of gender is specific. In this category, the verbal constructions indicate masculine (he ran), feminine (she ran), and neuter (it ran) genders.

So the third person singular in English is unusual. It is the only form that can specify gender. But remember, that which is most common is also the most irregular; and the third person singular is the most frequent form of the verb in any language, English and Hebrew included.

HEBREW VERB CONJUGATIONS

Most of the information above also applies to the conjugation of Hebrew verbs. However, the correspondence is not always one to one. Recognizing these differences early on should take some of the sting out of learning Hebrew. Remember, you know the basic grammatical principles for English. You must now learn how to apply these principles in the context of the Hebrew verb. Some of the more significant differences are summarized below.

The first major difference is simply one of presentation. In the English verb conjugation, the verbs are presented in the order of first, second, and third persons (1, 2, 3), singular and then plural. In Hebrew, however, the arrangement is third, second, and first person (3, 2, 1), singular and then plural (see, for example, *BBH* 13.5). In other words, when compared with English, the presentation by person in the Hebrew conjugation is reversed. No problem. Remember the alphabet. It's backwards too. Hey, if you grew up suffering from dyslexia, this will actually make sense.

A second major difference in conjugation patterns stems from the relationship between person and gender. In the

English verb system, the first and second persons are common in gender, but the third person (singular) specifies gender as masculine, feminine, or neuter. In the Hebrew verb system, the first person is still common, just like English. The second person, however, is not common, but rather specifies gender as either masculine or feminine. In other words, there are two different forms for the word "you" in Hebrew; one is masculine and one is feminine (*BBH* 13.5; 15.3). The third person is once again the most irregular. In English, the third person specifies gender as masculine, feminine, or neuter. In the Hebrew verb system, however, some third person forms are common (*BBH* 13.6.2), but others specify gender as masculine or feminine (*BBH* 15.4.5). Oy vey, the third person!

A third major difference between the English and Hebrew verb conjugations is the way in which each system encodes person, gender, and number. In the English verb conjugation, the use of a personal pronoun in the subjective case is required in most instances, as illustrated by the following examples: "*I* ran," "*you* ran," "*they* ran." In Hebrew, however, personal pronouns are not required. Rather, the form of the verb itself provides this information to the reader, often by means of particular prefixes and/or suffixes attached to the verb. In English, this type of distinction can occur in certain third person singular verbs. For example, note the difference in the form of the verbs in "you run" and "he runs" or in "I sleep" and "she sleeps." In both cases, the third person forms, "he runs" and "she sleeps," require the addition of the letter *s* to the end of the verb. This is similar to how Hebrew works to indicate person, gender, and number, but in a much more pervasive way (*BBH* 13.5; 15.3; 18.3). Just remember, what English does with pronouns, Hebrew does with verbal prefixes and suffixes.

EXERCISES

In the following sentences, the verbs appear in italics. For each verb, identify the person, gender, number, and tense. This particular type of exercise is called parsing (*BBH* 12.5; 13.11; 15.8). You will do it often in Hebrew.

1. God *created* the heavens.

2. The women *wept* for Naomi.

3. The land *produced* vegetation on the third day.

4. Cain *killed* his brother.

5. We *will worship* the Lord.

6. The birds of the air *will eat* your flesh.

7. The fool *says*, "There *is* no God."

8. Joshua *inquired* of the Lord.

9. You (all) *have transgressed* the covenant of the Lord.

10. Eve *was* the mother of all living.

11

VOICE AND ACTION:
Understanding Verb Verbalization

INTRODUCTION

Okay, this is the last chapter intended to provide a basic introduction to verbs. In chapter 9, we covered mood, tense, and aspect. Then, in chapter 10, we covered person, gender, and number. Now, in this chapter, we will cover the topics of voice and action as they relate to verbs.

The categories of voice and action are closely related. At their core, they help us to understand the nature of verbal action. For example, some verbs express actions that move away from the verbal subject, while other verbs express actions that move toward the verbal subject. In addition to the direction of a verb's action, there are also different types of action. Some actions are simple, while others are intensive or causative. You probably already know this, at least at the intuitive level.

VERBAL VOICE

Verbs don't really "say" anything. They don't even have vocal chords, except perhaps on Sesame Street. Rather, a verb's **voice** characterizes the relationship between the verbal action and the subject of that action. For our purposes, we will consider the following three categories of verbal voice: active, passive, and reflexive.

With the **active voice**, the subject of the verb performs the action of the verb. In other words, the verbal action moves out, or away from, the verbal subject. In the following examples, the verbs are active:

> Moses *struck down* the Egyptian.
>
> David *loved* Bathsheba.
>
> Elijah *mocked* the prophets of Baal.

With the **passive voice**, the subject of the verb receives the verbal action. Think of the passive voice as the opposite of the active voice. In the active voice, the action moves away from the subject, but with the passive voice, the action moves toward the subject. In the following examples, the verbs are passive:

> Moses *was struck down* by the Egyptian.
>
> David *was loved* by Bathsheba.
>
> Elijah *was mocked* by the prophets of Baal.

Notice that, in each of the above examples, the passive voice in English is formed with the addition of a form of the verb "to be." So, "struck" is active, but "*was* struck" is passive. The addition of "was" to "struck" changed the voice of the verb from active to passive.

You may have also noticed that the direct objects in the active sentences above (the Egyptian, Bathsheba, and the prophets of Baal) became prepositional phrases in the passive sentence constructions (by the Egyptian, by Bathsheba, and by the prophets of Baal). This is a common pattern in passive verb constructions. The prepositional phrases in these sentences identify the new agent of the verbal action. In the active example, "David loved Bathsheba," David performs the verbal action and Bathsheba receives the verbal action. However, in the passive example, "David was loved by Bathsheba," David now receives the verbal action performed by Bathsheba.

Let's put this another way. It may help. Study the following two sentences:

Elijah was mocked by the prophets of Baal.
The prophets of Baal mocked Elijah.

What's the difference between these two sentences? In both sentences, Elijah is mocked. Additionally, the prophets of Baal are the mockers in both examples. Sure, the first example is active and the second is passive, but both examples express the same basic reality. The fundamental difference, therefore, is one of focus or topic.[1] In the first example, Elijah is the focus. In the second example, the prophets of Baal are the focus.

The last voice is the reflexive voice. With the **reflexive voice**, the subject of the verb performs *and* receives the verbal action. Think of the reflexive voice as a combination of the active and passive voices. In the active voice, the action moves away from the subject, but with the passive voice, the action moves toward the subject. With the reflexive voice,

---

1.   In the study of language, a science called "linguistics," the labels "topic" and "focus" are used to describe that which is prominent in the sentence. They identify what the sentence is about.

however, the action of the verb moves both away from and back toward the verbal subject. In the following examples, the verbs are reflexive:

> Moses *struck* himself.
> Bathsheba *loved* herself.
> The prophets of Baal *mocked* themselves.

Notice how, in each of the above examples, the reflexive voice in English is formed with an active verb followed by a reflexive pronoun. In these examples, the reflexive pronouns are "himself," herself," and "themselves." In English, you can remember that the *reflexive voice* and *reflexive pronouns* go together. You should also note that, with the reflexive voice, the reflexive pronoun functions as the object of the verb, whose antecedent is the verbal subject.

The following table summarizes the basic concepts associated with verbal voice.

Voice	Definition	Example
Active	Subject performs verbal action	Moses *struck* the Egyptian
Passive	Subject receives verbal action	Moses *was struck* by the Egyptian
Reflexive	Subject performs and receives verbal action	Moses *struck himself*

VERBAL ACTION

Verbs in any language are capable of expressing a variety of different types of action. For example, consider the verbs "to learn" and "to teach." The verb "to learn" expresses a simple action while the verb to teach expresses a causative type of action. In other words, "to teach" is "to *cause* someone to learn." Consider two more verbs: "to run" and "to sprint." The verb "to run" expresses a simple type of action while the verb "to sprint" describes an *intensified* form of running. Different languages portray different types of action in a variety of ways. Sometimes different verbs are used, like "run" and "sprint" or "rise" and "raise." In some languages, like Hebrew, the form of a particular verb itself may be altered to express these notions of action. For the purpose of studying Hebrew, we will discuss three basic types of action: simple, intensive, and causative.

Simple action is, well, simple. Think of this category of action as the base category from which all other actions are understood. Don't complicate the issue. It's *simple*.

Intensive action is "supersized" simple action. Instead of "breaking" the vase, you "smash" the vase into little pieces. Or, instead of walking through a room, you "pace back and forth" in that room. Instead of "being happy," you "make someone happy." These are all different types of intensive action. This stuff is *intense*!

Causative action is just that, causative, whereby the subject "causes" something to happen to someone or something else. For example, the causative equivalent of "to learn" is "to teach." So, if I *teach* Hebrew to Moses, then I *cause* Moses *to learn* Hebrew. For another example, the causative of "to eat" is "to feed." If Moses *feeds* the people in the wilderness, then he *causes* them *to eat*. Notice how we used the key word "cause" to indicate a causative type of action (e.g., "*cause* to learn" or "*cause* to eat"). Don't worry, there is no *cause* for alarm.

HEBREW ACTION HEROES

Okay, check this out. In Hebrew, the verbal categories of voice and action are closely related. Like English, Hebrew utilizes the active, passive, and reflexive voices. Hebrew also divides verbal action into the simple, intensive, and causative categories. In fact, the Hebrew verb system is structured by the realities of *voice* and *action*. The following chart illustrates this basic structure for the Hebrew verbal system.

	Simple	Intensive	Causative
Active	he broke	he smashed	he caused to break
Passive	he was broken	he was smashed	he was caused to break
Reflexive	he broke himself	he smashed himself	he was caused to break himself

In Hebrew, different types of action are indicated by the action heroes of the verb system, the so-called stems. You will get the chance to study the impact of verbal stems in Hebrew in *BBH* chapters 24–35 (see also *BBH* 12.5–9). For now, the following chart simply identifies which Hebrew verb stems indicate what voice and action.

	Simple	Intensive	Causative
Active	Qal Stem	Piel Stem	Hiphil Stem
Passive	Niphal Stem	Pual Stem	Hophal Stem
Reflexive	Niphal Stem	Hithpael Stem	

I know, these are really weird names. Who has ever heard of something called "Niphal" or "Pual." Don't worry, these things are explained in your Hebrew grammar. For now, charts like this serve as points of reference and a means for identifying English and Hebrew correspondence. Note how English and Hebrew share in common issues of voice and action. The difference between the two languages is simply how these realities are expressed. In Hebrew, the action hero *stems* are used.

EXERCISES

In the following sentences, selected verbs appear in italics. For each verb, identify its voice as either **active, passive,** or **reflexive**.

1. The word of the LORD *came* to Jonah.

2. The word of the LORD *was given* to Jonah.

3. Your brother Esau is *consoling himself* with the thought of killing you.

4. There he *built* an altar, and he *called* the place El Bethel, because it was there that God *revealed himself* to him when he *was fleeing* from his brother.

5. Joseph *threw himself* upon his father and *wept* over him and *kissed* him.

6. If, however, the woman has not *defiled herself* and is free from impurity, she *will be cleared* of guilt.

7. The fool *says*, "There is no God."

8. But to Hannah he *gave* a double portion because he *loved* her, and the LORD *had closed* her womb.

9. But for Adam no suitable helper *was found*.

10. When the LORD saw that Leah *was not loved*, he *opened* her womb.

IMPERATIVE:
Clause Commandos

INTRODUCTION

Frequently, my wife and I buckle the kids into the minivan, head up the Natchez Trace Parkway, and listen to a recorded sermon. Our children definitely have their preferences when it comes to sermon selection. One of our favorite nonlocal pastors speaks with a certain level of unction that translates into an escalating volume of delivery and frequent imperatives. Another one of our favorites is more conversational in tone, lingering in explanation and contextualization. Without exception, our children prefer the more conversational delivery system.

In the Bible, both approaches are accounted for. There is both the "indicative," which requires explanation, and the "imperative," which requires obedience. For example, in

Exodus 20:2, it is recorded that Yahweh brought up Israel out of Egypt. This is an indicative statement that requires explanation. It is a statement of fact. A few verses later, in Exodus 20:12, the people of God are commanded to honor their fathers and mothers. This is a command that requires obedience (as well as explanation). It is an imperative statement. In this chapter, we move out of the indicative mood and into the imperative mood.[1]

THE ENGLISH COMMANDO

Back in chapter 9, the imperative mood was described as the mood of commands and requests. Commands are stronger than requests, and requests range from urgent to polite. Positive commands are called **admonitions** and negative commands are labeled as **prohibitions**. The major player in the imperative mood is the **imperative verb**. Think of the imperative verb as the "commando" of the verbal word. The imperative verb is the verb that makes things happen.

In English, the imperative verbal form is derived from the infinitive form without "to." For example, the infinitive form is "*to* study," and the imperative form is simply "study." Just get rid of the "to" and you have the imperative verbal form in English.

Additionally, the imperative verb is always second person, as in "you." In most cases, however, the presence of the pronoun is not required to make sense of the command. In fact, the pronoun is normally absent. For example, in a command like, "(you) honor your father and mother," the pro-

------

1.   For the imperative mood, some grammarians will use the nomenclature "volitional" or "projective" modality.

noun "you" is not required, but it is always implied. The imperative verb is the only verb in English that does not require a noun or personal pronoun in order to identify the subject.

It is also helpful to remember that the English pronoun "you" is both masculine and feminine, singular and plural. It is the personal pronoun with the most comprehensive scope of reference. It can refer to one man or one woman. It can refer to a group of men or a group of women. The pronoun "you" can even refer to a single group consisting of both women and men. In the southern U.S., they have worked out some of this ambiguity in the colloquialism "y'all" as a substitute for the standard second person plural pronoun. Y'all understand?

HEBREW COMMANDOS

The Hebrew commando verb is also called the "imperative," and it is also second person (*BBH* 18). There are, however, two major differences between the Hebrew and English imperative systems.

The first major difference is that the Hebrew imperative is inflected for gender and number (*BBH* 18.3–4). This means that there are four different forms of the Hebrew imperative verb, each of which encodes the gender and number for the second person (2ms, 2fs, 2mp, 2fp). Now, you might think that having four different forms of the imperative is a disadvantage to the Hebrew system, but it isn't. Sure, it does add to the madness of paradigm memorization, but it pays off by providing greater specificity. In Hebrew, you always know the gender and number of the person or group addressed by the second person imperative.

The second major difference is that you cannot negate the Hebrew imperative (*BBH* 18.5). In English, we can use the imperative for both admonitions and prohibitions. We can say, both "*Worship* the Lᴏʀᴅ" (admonition) and "*Do not worship* other gods" (prohibition). The Hebrew imperative is used exclusively for positive commands or admonitions. An entirely different construction is used for Hebrew prohibitions. So, for example, in Exodus 20, there are sixteen different commands (admonitions and prohibitions) that make up the so-called ten commandments. Just one of these sixteen commands is an actual imperative verb, the command to "honor" father and mother.

OTHER COMMANDS

You now know that imperative verbs are always second person in both English and Hebrew. But what if you want to boss other people around too? Are there commands for the first and third persons? The answer, of course, is "yes." In English, commands of this type are constructed with key words like "must" or "let." For example, the sentence, "we *must* understand English grammar," is a type of command or exhortation in the first person. Similarly, "*let* him study Hebrew," is a third person example. Notice how the key words "let" and "must" are use in these English examples.

Hebrew also has the ability to express volition in the first and third persons. This is done with first (*BBH* 18.3) and third (*BBH* 18.4) person imperfect verbs. Commands of this type are marked in Hebrew by the position of the verb in its clause (word order) and, sometimes, by the form of the verb itself (morphology). English and Hebrew can do the same thing. They just do it in different ways.

EXERCISES

Circle the imperative verbs in the following English sentences.

1. God blessed them and said, "Be fruitful and increase in number and fill the water in the seas."

2. The LORD had said to Abram, "Leave your country, your people and your father's household and go to the land I will show you."

3. The LORD said to Moses, "Chisel out two stone tablets like the first ones, and I will write on them the words that were on the first tablets, which you broke."

4. Remember the days of old; consider the generations long past. Ask your father and he will tell you, your elders, and they will explain to you.

5. Wake up, wake up, Deborah! Wake up, wake up, break out in song! Arise, O Barak! Take captive your captives.

6. Give thanks to the LORD, call on his name; make known among the nations what he has done, and proclaim that his name is exalted.

7. Guard the fortress, watch the road, brace yourselves, marshal all your strength!

8. Write down the revelation and make it plain on tablets so that a herald may run with it.

9. Look on me and answer, O LORD my God. Give light to my eyes, or I will sleep in death.

10. Sing to the LORD, praise his name; proclaim his salvation day after day.

13

INFINITIVES:
To Be or Not To Be, That Is the Infinitive!

INTRODUCTION

In the exciting and provocative world of grammar, it is not uncommon to distinguish nouns and nominals from verbs and verbals. In general, nouns name things and verbs describe actions or states of being. Verbs are the movers and shakers of the grammatical world and nouns are those things that move and shake. Some words, however, just can't make up their mind.

The English infinitive is one of these undecided types of words. We define the infinitive as a **verbal noun** because it has both verbal and nominal characteristics. It looks like a verb, but it functions more like a noun. You can think of the infinitive as a word that maintains dual citizenship in both the nominal and verbal worlds.

ENGLISH INFINITIVE

The English infinitive normally appears as a combination of "to" plus the basic or dictionary form of a verb, such as "to study," "to learn," or "to worship." It is the simplest of verbs, not inflected for person, gender, number, tense (time), or aspect (type of action).

Like verbs, infinitives can take subjects, objects, and modifiers. Like nouns, however, infinitives can function as verbal subjects, objects, or modifiers. Confusing? Let's look at some examples in order to make some sense of this.

Our first example is a well-known quote from the English poet Alexander Pope (1688–1744): "To err is human, to forgive is divine." In this example, the infinitives "to err" and "to forgive" function as the subjects of their respective clauses, just like a noun would function.

Our second example will use the infinitive as the object of a finite verb: "I love to study." In this example, the infinitive "to study" is the object of the verb "love." Note how, in this case, the infinitive can be replaced with a regular noun, such as "Hebrew," as in "I love Hebrew." Both the infinitive "to study" and the noun "Hebrew" function as the object of the verb "love." The infinitive and the noun share functions.

Now, let's go one step further with this second example. Let's consider, "I love to study Hebrew in the morning." Here again, the infinitive "to study" is the object of the verb "love." It is functioning just like a noun would function. But like a verb, the infinitive "to study" takes it's own object, "Hebrew," and modifier, "in the morning." So, in this single example, you can see just how an infinitive might exhibit both verbal and nominal qualities at the very same time. As a verb, the infinitive "to study" denotes action, but it functions like a noun within its sentence as the object of the main verb, "love."

Let's consider one final example of the English infinitive. The example is, "Hardy studies Hebrew (in order) to glorify God." The subject of the verb "studies" is "Hardy" and its object is "Hebrew." Following the verbal object is the infinitive phrase "to glorify God." In this case, the infinitive modifies the verb "studies." It tells us why Hardy studies. This use of the infinitive is adverbial because, like an adverb, it modifies a verb. In this particular case, the key words "in order" may be used with the infinitive construction to specify just how the infinitive phrase is intended to modify the main verb, denoting purpose.

By way of quick review, remember the following four things about the English infinitive:

1. The English infinitive is a verbal noun. It does not encode person, gender, number, tense (time), or aspect (type of action).

2. Like a verb, the infinitive describes an action (to study) or state of being.

3. Like a verb, the infinitive can take objects and modifiers (to study *Hebrew in the morning*).

4. Though it may look and feel like a verb, the infinitive functions more like a noun – as a verbal subject (*to err* is human), or as a verbal object (I love *to study*).

HEBREW INFINITIVES

Notice in the heading just above this line that I have used the plural form "infinitives," and not the singular form "infinitive." This is because, in Hebrew, there are two different infinitives: the **Infinitive Construct** (*BBH* 20) and **Infinitive Absolute** (*BBH* 21). Both of the Hebrew infinitives are classified as verbal nouns, but it is the Infinitive Construct that more closely corresponds to our English infinitive. Like

the English infinitive, the Hebrew Infinitive Construct frequently appears with the preposition "to" (Hebrew לְ)[1] and
functions in many of the same ways. The Infinitive Absolute,
however, never appears with the preposition "to." Neither
does it correspond in function. So, when it comes to the
infinitive, remember that the English infinitive and the
Hebrew Infinitive Construct are closely related. The Hebrew
Infinitive Absolute is more of a distant relative, like your
crazy cousin Willy.

EXERCISES

Circle the infinitive verbal constructions in the following English sentences. In each case, try and identify how the
infinitive is being used.

1. God set them in the expanse of the sky to give light
   on the earth, to govern the day and the night, and to
   separate light from darkness. And God saw that it
   was good.

2. The LORD God took the man and put him in the Garden of Eden to work it and to take care of it.

3. The LORD went ahead of you on your journey, in fire
   by night and in a cloud by day, to search out places
   for you to camp and to show you the way you
   should go.

4. But Ruth said, "Do not urge me to leave you or to
   turn back from following you; for where you go, I
   will go, and where you lodge, I will lodge."

---

1. The Infinitive Construct occurs 6,951 times in the Hebrew
Bible. It appears with the English equivalent of "to" (Hebrew לְ)
4,508 times, or 65% of the time.

5. Behold, to obey is better than sacrifice, and to heed
   is better than the fat of rams.

6. The words of his mouth are wicked and deceitful; he
   has ceased to be wise and to do good.

7. To praise the LORD is good, and to make music to
   your name, O Most High, to proclaim your love in
   the morning.

8. The teaching of the wise is a fountain of life, to turn
   aside from the snares of death.

9. To show partiality to the wicked is not good, nor to
   thrust aside the righteous in judgment.

10. There is a time to give birth and a time to die; a time
    to plant and a time to uproot what is planted; a time
    to kill and a time to heal; a time to tear down and a
    time to build up; a time to weep and a time to laugh;
    a time to mourn and a time to dance; a time to throw
    stones and a time to gather stones; a time to embrace
    and a time to shun embracing; a time to search and a
    time to give up as lost; a time to keep and a time to
    throw away; a time to tear apart and a time to sew
    together; a time to be silent and a time to speak; a
    time to love and a time to hate; a time for war and a
    time for peace.

14

PARTICIPLES:
Those Verbs That End with -ING

INTRODUCTION

In the previous chapter, we described infinitives as verbal nouns, or words having dual citizenship in both the verbal and the nominal worlds. Like infinitives, participles share this status of dual citizenship. But participles are not verbal nouns. Rather, participles are **verbal adjectives**. This means that participles look and feel like a verb, describing some sort of action, but function more like an adjective. Once again, it is a word that just can't make up its mind. Is it a verb? Is it an adjective? Yes, it's a participle!

ENGLISH PARTICIPLE

So what does an English participle look like? Well, this will depend on the type of participle. In English there are two basic forms of the participle: the present participle form and the past participle form.

Present participles are normally formed by adding "ing" to the basic form of the verb. Examples of the English present participle include "studying," "writing," and "praying."

Past participles are a little more eclectic in their formation. Most of the English past participles are formed by adding either "ed" or "en" to the basic form of the word. Examples of the English past participle include "cursed," "blessed," "written," and "eaten." There are other English verbs that form the past participle by changing the verb stem, usually, but not exclusively, the stem vowel. For example, the present participle form of "sing" is "singing," but the past participle form is "sung" (not "singed"). With the form "sung," no "ed" or "en" is added. Rather, the stem vowel was changed (*i* to *u*) in this verb to indicate the past participle. "Sing" became "sung." There is a song in this!

The following chart summarizes the basic forms of the English participle. This chart may be of some assistance when you begin translating Hebrew participles.

English Infinitive	Present Participle	Past Participle
to study	studying	studied
to write	writing	written
to bless	blessing	blessed
to curse	cursing	cursed
to eat	eating	eaten
to sing	singing	sung

Okay, we have answered the question, what do English participles look like? The next question to answer is, what do these participles communicate? The answer to this question is, not much. In fact, it is more instructive to ask, what don't participles tell us about verbal action? Like the English infinitive, participles are **nonfinite verbs**. This means that they don't normally take subjects, and so they are not inflected for person, gender, or number. Additionally, by themselves, participles do not indicate tense (time of action), aspect (type of action), or mood (indicative, imperative, subjunctive). They depend on other verbs in their shared context to communicate these realities.

You now know that English participles have only two basic forms (present and past), and that they are limited in the expression of standard verbal realities by their nonfinite verbal status. Do not be fooled, though. These limitations make the participle an extremely flexible part of speech, capable of performing a variety of functions in the English language. In this chapter, we will highlight only those uses of the English participle that will help us later to understand Hebrew participles.

English participles can be used **attributively**, like an adjective, to modify a noun. In the following examples, present participles appear in the left column and past participles appear in the right column.

the *writing* prophet	the *written* word
the *ruling* king	the *cursed* slave
the *running* water	the *blessed* woman

English participles can be used **predicatively**, in the formation of predications, normally in conjunction with a form of the verb "to be." In the following examples, present participles appear in the left column with a present tense form of the verb "to be" and past participles appear in the right column with a past tense form of the verb "to be."

the prophet is *writing*	the word was *written*
the king is *ruling*	the slave was *cursed*
the water is *running*	the woman was *blessed*

Finally, English participles can be used **substantively**, like a noun. Now, in all truth, when "participles" are used this way, they are sometimes called **gerunds** in English. In all of the biblical languages, however, participles perform this function, and so we just lump them together. There are many ways in which participles (gerunds) perform the function of a noun. Some of the more common uses include verbal subject, verbal object, and object of the preposition.

ruling is for kings	*writing* is for prophets
the king enjoyed *ruling*	the prophet detested *writing*
the king ruled with a *blessing*	after *blessing*, the priest ate

You might have noticed from your study of adjectives, that participles and adjectives share the same three basic functions: attributive, predicative, and substantive. This stems from the adjectival nature of the participle. So remember, whatever an adjective can do, the participle can do too.

HEBREW PARTICIPLE

There are many similarities between the Hebrew participle and the English participle (and gerund). They are both nonfinite verbs. They are both verbal adjectives (*BBH* 22.1), and they both share the same basic functions (*BBH* 22.5; 22.9).

There are, however, a few differences worth noting. The first difference pertains to gender and number. The English participle does not inflect for gender or number, just like the

English adjective. The Hebrew participle, on the other hand, does inflect for *both* gender *and* number, just like the Hebrew adjective (*BBH* 22.2–3, 5). This simply means that participles will match the words they modify, or refer to, in the categories of gender and number. If, for example, a Hebrew participle is modifying a masculine plural noun (ending in -*im*), then the corresponding participle will also be masculine and plural (ending in -*im*). If, for another example, a Hebrew participle is modifying a feminine plural noun (ending in -*ot*), then the corresponding participle will also be feminine and plural (ending in -*ot*). When it comes to matching, the Hebrew participle is one big copycat.

A second difference between the English and Hebrew participle systems is the existence of the Hebrew **passive participle** (see, for example, *BBH* 22.6–9). Technically speaking, English does not have a separate participle form for the expression of the passive voice. This reality appears in English as a combination of the English past participle and a form of the verb "to be," as in "being written" or "being blessed." Hebrew, on the other hand, has its own unique form for the passive participle construction (*BBH* 22.7).

There is one final difference between English and Hebrew participles that is worth noting. A few Hebrew participles were used substantively (as English gerunds) with such regularity that they became nouns (BBH 22.5.3). Examples of this phenomenon in Hebrew include the nouns commonly translated as "priest," "judge," "enemy," and "redeemer." So, "the judging one" simply became the "judge," or "the redeeming one" became, over time, the "redeemer." You will be able to recognize these words in Hebrew by their formation (vowel pattern) as participles.

EXERCISES

Circle the participles in the following English sentences. In each case, try and identify how the participle is being used (attributive, predicative, substantive).

1. The Spirit of God was hovering over the waters.

2. Let the water teem with living creatures, and let birds fly above the earth across the expanse.

3. And God blessed the seventh day and made it holy, because on it he rested from all the work of creating that he had done.

4. The LORD God formed the man from the dust of the ground and breathed into his nostrils the breath of life, and the man became a living being.

5. And the LORD God made all kinds of trees grow out of the ground—trees that were pleasing to the eye and good for food.

6. So the LORD God caused the man to fall into a deep sleep; and while he was sleeping, he took one of the man's ribs and closed up the place with flesh.

7. When the woman saw that the fruit of the tree was good for food and pleasing to the eye, and also desirable for gaining wisdom, she took some and ate it.

8. Cursed are you above all the livestock and all the wild animals!

9. Blessed be Abram by God Most High, creator of heaven and earth. And blessed be God Most High, who delivered your enemies into your hand.

10. When the LORD saw that Leah was hated, he opened her womb, but Rachel was barren.

Glossary of Terms

abjad An alphabetic writing system without vowels (e.g., Hebrew, Aramaic, and Arabic alphabets).

abstract A noun naming a person, place, or thing that cannot be perceived by the senses (e.g., faith, hope, love).

active One of three voices used by verbs. In the active voice, the subject of the verb performs the action of the verb (e.g., Moses struck the rock).

adjectival A term used to describe any type of word, phrase, or clause that modifies a noun.

adjective A word that modifies, describes, characterizes, or classifies a noun (e.g., *good* book, *big* dog, *nice* smile).

admonition A positive command, something to do (e.g., honor your father and mother).

adverbial A term used to describe any type of word, phrase, or clause that modifies a verb.

affix   A generic term for either a prefix or a suffix.

alphabet   A system of writing in which a single sign or symbol represents a single sound (e.g., English, Latin, Greek, and Cyrillic alphabets).

antecedent   A word substituted or replaced by a pronoun. A pronoun's antecedent is the noun that the pronoun replaced.

article   The English definite article is "the" and it particularizes a noun (e.g., *the* book). The English indefinite article, "a" or "an," is used for generic or nonparticular nouns (*a* book, *an* apple).

aspect   The way a verb portrays action: simple (default), perfect (completed action), progressive (ongoing action), past progressive (ongoing action in the past).

attributive   An adjectival or participial function in which the adjective or participle directly modifies a noun (e.g. *good* dog, *running* water).

case   A term used to refer to how nouns function. The English cases are subjective, objective, and possessive. The same cases or noun functions occur in Hebrew.

causative   A type of verbal action in which the subject causes something to happen to someone or something (e.g., Moses fed the Israelites, i.e., he caused them to eat).

clause
: A group of words containing a subject and a predicate. Clauses can be independent and dependent, main or subordinate.

collective
: A noun singular in number but referring to more than one person or thing as a single entity (e.g., people, team, family, group).

common
: A common noun is a generic noun, not referring to any specific person, place, or thing. Common gender refers to a noun or verb whose reference can be either masculine or feminine.

conjunction
: A word used to join other words, phrases, or clauses within a sentence (e.g., and, but, or, so, for, yet).

concrete
: A noun naming a person, place, or thing that can be perceived by the senses (e.g., rock, staff, horse).

demonstrative
: The English demonstratives are this, these, that, and those. They can function as adjectives (*this* book) or pronouns (*that* is my book).

diphthong
: A combination of two vowels pronounced as a single vowel sound (e.g., "ei" in "either").

first
: First person pronouns or verbs are used when the speaker or writer is the subject of the idea or verbal action (e.g., *my* book, *I* write).

gender   A grammatical category referring to different patterns of verb and noun inflection (grammatical gender), or to items that actually have physical gender, such as male or female (natural gender).

gerund   A verb ending in *-ing* but functioning like a noun. In Hebrew, substantive participles perform this function.

indicative   One of three moods used by verbs. The indicative mood is used to describe reality or to ask questions (e.g., The book is red. Is the book red?).

infinitive   The English infinitive is a verbal noun, not inflected for person, gender, or number. Like a verb, it describes an action or state of being, taking objects and modifiers. In spite of these verbal qualities, the infinitive functions more like a noun or modifier.

intensive   A type of verbal action that amplifies the simple type of action (e.g., "to break" becomes "to smash or "to run" becomes "to sprint").

interrogative   A pronoun used in the formation of questions. The English interrogative pronouns include who, whom, what, which, and whose (e.g., *Who* studies grammar?).

imperative   One of three moods used by verbs. The imperative mood is used when the speaker desires to change reality (e.g., Shut the door!). The imperative verb is the main verb used for the imperative mood.

logography A system of writing in which a single sign or symbol represents a single word (e.g., traditional Chinese, ancient Egyptian hieroglyphics).

mood A verb's portrayal of reality. The indicative mood is used to describe reality. The imperative mood is used to when the speaker desires to change reality. The subjunctive mood is used to portray possible or probable realities.

noun A part of speech used to name a person, place, thing, or idea. Nouns can be concrete or abstract, singular or plural, definite or indefinite, common or proper.

number A grammatical category referring to the number of items indicated by a noun or verb, singular or plural. The singular number refers to one item. The plural number refers to more than one item. Hebrew also has the dual number, referring specifically to two items.

object A direct object is the person or thing that directly receives the action of the verb. An indirect object is the person or thing that indirectly receives the action of the verb. It designates "to whom or what" or "for whom or what" the verbal action is performed.

objective Functioning as the object of a verb or preposition. A noun may be either the direct or indirect object of the verb.

participle   The English participle is a verbal adjective, not inflected for person, gender, or number. Like a verb, it describes an action or state of being, taking objects and modifiers. In spite of these verbal qualities, the participle functions more like an adjective (attributive, predicative, and substantive).

passive   One of three voices used by verbs. In the passive voice, the subject of the verb receives the action of the verb (e.g., Moses was struck).

perfective   One of four English verb aspects. The perfective aspect characterizes the verbal action as completed, viewed from without, as a whole.

phrase   A group of words lacking a subject and predicate, such as a prepositional phrase.

possessive   A possessive noun shows possession or is in the possessive case, usually by adding 's to the noun (e.g., *David's* sling, *Goliath's* sword). A possessive pronoun also shows possession (*his* sling, *her* sword).

predicate   The part of the sentence containing the verb and stating something about the subject. A predicate nominative is a noun that functions as the "object" of the verb "to be," as in "The Lord is *God*." A predicate adjective is an adjective that functions as the "object" of the verb "to be," as in "The Lord is *good*."

predicative   A predicative adjective or participle is an adjective or participle that functions as the object of the verb "to be" (e.g., my hair is *red*, the dog is *running*).

prefix   Something added to the beginning of a word (e.g., *a*moral, *re*invent, *in*ability). See affix.

preposition   A word or group of words used to describe relationships between other words (e.g., above, under, on, over, before, after, in the presence of, on account of). A prepositional phrase consists of a preposition and its object (e.g., in the morning, after dinner).

prohibition   A negative command, something not to do (e.g., do not steal).

projective   An alternate designation for the imperative mood. Also called volitional.

progressive   One of four English verb aspects. The progressive aspect characterizes the verbal action as an ongoing process, viewed from within, not as a whole. In addition to the present progressive aspect, there is also the past progressive aspect, whereby the ongoing action is located in the past.

pronoun   A word that replaces or substitutes for another noun. Categories of English pronouns include personal (e.g., he, she, it), demonstrative (e.g., this, these), relative (e.g., who, that, which), and interrogative (e.g., who?, what?).

proper   A proper noun is a particular noun, referring to a specific person, place, or thing (e.g., Moses, Egypt, Israel).

reflexive   One of three voices used by verbs. In the reflexive voice, the subject of the verb both performs and receives the action of the verb (e.g., Moses struck himself).

relative   A relative pronoun introduces a relative clause, which normally modifies a noun (e.g., the dog *that* ate my homework). The English relative pronouns include that, who, whom, whose, what, which.

second   Second person pronouns or verbs are used for those people or groups directly addressed by the verbal subject (e.g., *your* book, *you* write).

sentence   A sentence consists of at least one independent clause, but may contain any number of independent or dependent clauses, as well as phrases.

simple   One of four English verb aspects. The simple aspect is the undefined or default aspect. It simply communicates that the verbal action took place.

subject   A noun, pronoun, or noun phrase about which a clause makes a statement. With passive verbs, the subject receives the verbal action as the goal or target of verbal action.

subjective   A subjective noun is a noun that functions as
                  the subject of a verb. It is in the subjective
                  (nominative) case.

subjunctive   One of three moods used by verbs. The sub-
                  junctive mood is used to portray possible or
                  probable realities (e.g., he might study
                  Hebrew).

substantive   A substantive adjective or participle is an
                  adjective or participle that functions like a
                  noun (e.g. *red* is my favorite color, *running*
                  hurts my legs). In English, the substantive
                  use of a participle is called a gerund.

suffix   Something added to the ending of a word
                  (e.g., dog*s*, kick*ed*, kick*ing*). Also called affix.

syllable   A combination of consonant and / or vowel
                  sounds that combine in a recognizable
                  manner to form words.

syllabary   A system of writing in which a single sign or
                  symbol represents a single syllable (e.g.,
                  ancient Akkadian).

tense   A term used with the indicative verb system
                  to denote the time of verbal action: past,
                  present, or future.

third   Third person pronouns or verbs are used for
                  those people or groups not directly
                  addressed by the verbal subject (e.g., *his*
                  book, *she* writes).

verb   Word used to portray an action or state of being.

verbless   A verbless clause is a clause that lacks a verb. This reality occurs frequently in Hebrew, but rarely in English.

voice   A term used to characterize the relationship between verbal action and the subject of that action. The three main voices are active, passive, and reflexive.

volitional   An alternate designation for the imperative mood. Also called projective.

word   An assembly of letters into a meaningful unit.